GOD'S GRACE TO YOU

GOD'S GRACE TO YOU

Charles
SPURGEON

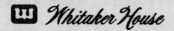 Whitaker House

All Scripture quotations are taken from the *King James Version* (KJV) of the Holy Bible.

GOD'S GRACE TO YOU

ISBN: 0-88368-432-2
Printed in the United States of America
Copyright © 1997 by Whitaker House

Whitaker House
30 Hunt Valley Circle
New Kensington, PA 15068

Library of Congress Cataloging-in-Publication Data

Spurgeon, C. H. (Charles Haddon), 1834–1892.
    God's grace to you / Charles Spurgeon.
        p.   cm.
    ISBN 0-88368-432-2 (pbk.)
    1. Covenants—Religious aspects—Christianity. 2. Christian life—
Baptist authors. 3. Grace (Theology) I. Title.
BT155.S65   1997
231.7 ' 6—dc21   97-38666

1 2 3 4 5 6 7 8 9 10 11 12 / 07 06 05 04 03 02 01 00 99 98 97

Contents

Chapter 1

The Wondrous Covenant

*For this is the covenant that I will make with the
house of Israel after those days, saith the Lord;
I will put my laws into their mind, and write them in
their hearts: and I will be to them a God,
and they shall be to me a people.
—Hebrews 8:10*

The doctrine of the divine covenant lies at the root of all true theology. It has been said that the person who understands the distinction between the covenant of works and the covenant of grace is a master of divinity. I am persuaded that most of the mistakes that men make concerning the doctrines of Scripture are based upon fundamental errors with regard to the covenants of law and of grace. May God grant me the power to impart instruction on this vital subject, and may He give you the grace to receive it.

In the order of history, so far as this world is concerned, the human race first stood in subjection to God under the covenant of works. Adam was the representative man. A certain law was given to him. If he kept it, he and all his posterity would be blessed as the result of obedience. If he broke it, he would incur the curse himself and subject all those represented by him to the same curse. Our first father broke that covenant. He fell; he failed to fulfill his obligations.

In his fall, Adam involved us all, for all people descended from him and all were physically present in his seed, just as Levi *"payed tithes in Abraham, for he was yet in the loins of his father, when Melchisedec met him"* (Hebrews 7:9–10). The first Adam thus represented us before God in the Fall. Our ruin, then, was complete before we were ever born. We were ruined by the failure of the first Adam, who stood as our first representative. To be saved by the works of the law is now impossible, for under that covenant we are already lost. If we are to be saved at all, it must be according to quite a different plan, not under the plan of doing and being rewarded for it. That has been tried, and the representative man upon whom it was tried has failed for us all. We have all failed in his failure; it is hopeless, therefore, to expect to win divine favor by anything that we can do or to merit divine blessing by way of reward.

However, divine mercy has intervened and provided a plan of salvation from the Fall. That plan is another covenant, a covenant God the Father made with His Son Jesus Christ, who is appropriately called the Second Adam because He also stood as the representative of men.

As far as Christ was concerned, the second covenant was quite as much a covenant of works as the first one was. The plan went something like this: Christ was to come into the world and perfectly obey the divine law. Inasmuch as the first Adam had broken the law, He was also to suffer the penalty of sin. If He would do both of these, then all whom He represented would be blessed in His blessedness and saved because of His merit. Do you see that, until our Lord lived and died on this earth, it was a covenant of works on His part? He had certain works to perform; upon condition of His performance, certain blessings would be given to us.

Our Lord has kept that covenant. His part of it has been fulfilled to the last letter. There is no commandment that He has not honored; there is no penalty of the broken law that He has not endured. He became a servant and was *"obedient unto death, even the death of the cross"* (Philippians 2:8). He has thus done what the first Adam could not accomplish, and He has retrieved what the first Adam forfeited by his transgressions. He has established the covenant, and now it ceases to be a covenant of works, for the works have all been completed.

> Jesus did them, did them all,
> Long, long ago.

And now, what remains to be fulfilled of the covenant? On His part, God has solemnly pledged Himself to give undeserved favor to everyone whom Jesus represented on the cross. For all whom the

Savior died, there are stored up bountiful blessings that will be given to them, not through their works, but as the sovereign gift of the grace of God, according to His covenant promise by which they are saved.

Beloved, behold the hope of the sons of men. The hope of their saving themselves is forever crushed, for they are already lost. The hope of their being saved by works is a fallacious one, for they cannot keep the law; they have already broken it. Yet, there is a way of salvation opened that can be explained this way: whosoever believes in the Lord Jesus Christ receives and partakes of the bliss that Christ has bought. All the blessings that belong to the covenant of grace through the work of Christ will belong to every soul who believes in Jesus. Whoever *"worketh not, but* [rather] *believeth on him that justifieth the ungodly"* (Romans 4:5), unto that person will the blessing of the new covenant of grace be undoubtedly given.

I hope that this explanation is clear enough. If Adam had kept the law, we would have been blessed by his keeping it. He broke it, and we have been cursed through him. Now the Second Adam, Christ Jesus, has kept the law. Therefore, if we are believers, we are represented in Christ and blessed with the results of the obedience of Jesus Christ to His Father's will. Through the ancient Scriptures Christ said, *"Lo, I come...to do thy will, O God"* (Psalm 40:7–8). He has done that will, and the blessings of grace are now freely given to the sons of men.

Now, first we will reflect on the privileges of the covenant of grace as found in our wondrous text.

Secondly, I will direct your attention to the parties concerned in the covenant. This will be quite enough for consideration in this chapter, I am sure, because of the depth of the subject at hand.

THE PRIVILEGES OF THE COVENANT OF GRACE

The first privilege is that illumination of their minds will be given to as many as are interested in receiving it. *"I will put my laws into their mind."* By nature our minds are dark toward God's will. Conscience keeps up in us a sort of broken recollection of what God's will is. It is a monument of God's will, but it is often hardly legible. People do not care to read it; they are averse to what they read there. *"Their foolish heart was darkened"* (Romans 1:21) is the expression Scripture gives with regard to the mind of man.

However, the Holy Spirit is promised to those interested in the covenant. He will come upon their minds and shed light instead of darkness, illuminating them as to what the will of God is. The ungodly man has some degree of light, but it is merely intellectual. It is a light that he does not love. *"Men loved darkness rather than light, because their deeds were evil"* (John 3:19). Nevertheless, where the Holy Spirit comes, He floods the soul with a divine luster in which the soul delights and desires to participate to the fullest degree.

Beloved, the renewed man, the man who is under the covenant of grace, does not need to resort constantly to his Bible to learn what he ought to do, nor does he have to go to some fellow Christian to

11

ask instruction. For him, the law of God is no longer written just on a tablet of stone or on parchment or on paper; rather, the law is written upon his own mind and heart. There is now a divine, infallible Spirit dwelling within him who tells him right and wrong. By this Spirit, he speedily discerns between good and evil. No longer is he of those *"that call evil good, and good evil; that put darkness for light, and light for darkness; that put bitter for sweet, and sweet for bitter!"* (Isaiah 5:20). His mind is enlightened as to the true holiness and the true purity that God requires.

Just watch the people to whom this light comes. By nature some of them are deeply depraved. All of them are depraved, but by practice some of them become still further dark. Is it not marvelous that a poor heathen, who scarcely seemed to recognize the distinction between right and wrong before the Spirit of God entered his mind, has afterward received at once the light of a responsive and tender conscience without needing to be taught all the precepts individually? This new mind has led him to know what is right and to love it, to recognize evil and to shun it.

If you want to civilize the world, it must be by preaching the Gospel. If you want to have men well instructed as to right and wrong, it must be by this divine instruction that only the Spirit of God can impart. He says, *"I will put my laws into their mind."* Then, how blessedly He does this when He takes a man, who previously had loved evil and called it good, and sheds a divine ray of light into his soul in such a way that, from that time, the man cannot be perverse or obstinate, but submits himself willingly to the divine will. That is one of the first blessings of the covenant—the illumination of the understanding.

The next blessing is *"I will...write them in their hearts."* This is more than knowing the law— infinitely more. God is saying, "I Myself will write the law, not merely on their understandings, where it may guide them, but in their hearts, where it will lead them." Beloved, the Holy Spirit makes men love the will of God, delight in all in which God delights, and abhor what God abhors. It is well said in the text that God will do this, for certainly it is not what a man can do for himself. *"Can the Ethiopian change his skin, or the leopard his spots? then may ye also do good, that are accustomed to do evil"* (Jeremiah 13:23). A minister cannot do this for a person; although he may preach to the ear, he cannot write God's law on the heart.

I have marveled at the expression used in the text: *"I will...write them in their hearts."* To write *on* a heart must be difficult work, but to write *in* a heart, in the very center of the heart—who could do this but God? A man may cut his name in the bark of a tree, and there it will stand, the letters growing with the tree. But, to cut his name in the heart of the tree—how could he accomplish this? And yet, God divinely engraves His will and His law in the very heart and nature of man!

The notion the world has about Christian people is that we do not conform to certain customs because we are afraid of God's punishment; they think we would like to revel in the vanities of the world, but we do not do so because we might encounter the harsh penalties that the Almighty could justly impose on us. Sons of this age, you do not comprehend the mysterious work of the Spirit! He does nothing of this sort. He does not make the children of God to be slaves in fear of bondage, but He so changes the nature of men that they do not love what they once loved. They turn away with loathing from the things they once delighted in; they can no more indulge in the sins that were once pleasurable to them than an angel could plunge himself down and wallow in the mire with the swine. This is a gracious work of God, and this is a blessed covenant in which it is promised that we will be taught what is right, to know and love what is right, and to do what is right with willing minds and hearts.

I may be addressing someone reading this who has been saying, "I wish I could be saved." What do you mean by that? Do you mean that you wish you might escape from hell? I would rather you had another wish, namely, "Oh, that I could escape from sin! Oh, that I could be made pure! Oh, that my passions could be bridled! Oh, that my longings and my lusts could be changed!" If that is your wish, what a glorious Gospel I have to present to you. I do not come and command you, "Do this, but do not do that." Moses gave the commandments in that way, and the legalistic preacher speaks in that fashion. However, as an ambassador of Christ who is unveiling the covenant of grace, I write to you that Jesus Christ has done such a work for sinners that God now comes to them for Christ's sake, makes them see what is right, and by a divine work upon them

14

and in them makes them love holiness and follow after righteousness.

I consider this one of the greatest blessings that I could ever address. I would sooner be holy than happy, if the two things could be divorced. Were it possible for a man always to sorrow and yet to be pure, I would choose the sorrow if I might win purity. Beloved, to be free from the power of sin, to be made to love holiness, is true happiness. A man who is holy is at peace with the creation, and he is in harmony with God. It is impossible for that man to suffer for long. He may for a while endure suffering for his lasting good; but as certainly as God is happy, the person who is holy must be happy. This world is not so constituted that in the long run holiness goes with sorrow. In eternity God will show that to be pure is to be blessed, to be obedient to the divine will is to be eternally glorified. In writing to you, then, about these two blessings of the covenant, I have essentially presented to you the open kingdom of heaven, open to all whom God's grace looks upon with an eye of mercy.

The next blessing of the covenant is "*I will be to them a God.*" If anyone should ask me what this means, I might reply, "Give me a month to consider it." When I had considered the text for a month, I would ask for another month; when I had waited a year, I would ask for another; and when I had waited until I grew gray, I would still ask the postponement of any attempt to fully explain it until eternity.

"*I will be to them a God.*" Now, please understand that where the Spirit of God has come to teach you the divine will and make you love the divine will, what does God become to you? A father? Yes, a loving, tender Father. A shepherd? Yes, a watchful Guardian of His flock. A friend? Yes, *"a friend that sticketh closer than a brother"* (Proverbs 18:24). A rock? A hedge? A fortress? A high tower? A castle of defense? A home? A heaven? Yes, all of these and more. When the Lord said, *"I will be their God"* (Jeremiah 32:38), He said more than all of these put together, for *"I will be to them a God"* encompasses all gracious titles, all blessed promises, and all divine privileges.

"I will be to them a God" includes—and now I hesitate, for what I am writing about here is infinite, and the infinite embodies all blessings. Do you want provision? The cattle on a thousand hills are His (Psalm 50:10). It is nothing for Him to give; it will not impoverish Him; He will give to you like a God. Do you want comfort? He is the God of all consolation (2 Corinthians 1:3); He will comfort you like a God. Do you want guidance? There is infinite wisdom waiting at your beck and call: *"If any of you lack wisdom, let him ask of God, that giveth to all men liberally, and upbraideth not; and it shall be given him"* (James 1:5). Do you want strength? There is eternal power, the same that upholds the everlasting hills, waiting to strengthen you (Philippians 4:13). Do you want grace? He *"delighteth in mercy"* (Micah 7:18), and all His mercy is yours.

Every attribute of God belongs to His people who are in covenant with Him. All that God is or can be (and what is not included in that?); all that you can imagine; all that the angels have; all that heaven is; all that is in Christ, even the boundless fullness of the Godhead (Colossians 2:9)—all this belongs to you, if you are in covenant with God through Jesus Christ. How rich, how blessed, how majestic, how noble are those who are in covenant with God! You who are allied with heaven, infinity belongs to you! Lift up your head, O child of God, and rejoice in a promise that I cannot expound and you cannot explore. There I must leave it; it is too deep to comprehend; we strive in vain to fathom it.

Notice the next blessing: *"And they shall be to me a people."* All flesh belongs to God in a certain sense. All men are his by rights of creation, and He has an infinite sovereignty over them. But He looks down upon the sons of men, selects some, and says, "These are Mine; these will be My special people."

When the hymnwriter set to music the historic battle of the king of Navarre, who was fighting for his throne, he penned these lyrics:

> He looked upon the foemen,
>   And his glance was stern and high;
> He looked upon his people,
>   And the tear was in his eye.

And when the king saw some of the French in arms against him,

> Then out spoke gentle Henry,
>   "No Frenchman is my foe;
> Down, down, with every foreigner,
>   But let your brethren go."

The king took care of his people even if they were in rebellion against him. He had different thoughts toward them than he had toward others.

"Let them go," he seemed to say, "because they are my people." Therefore, take note that in the great battles and strife of this world, when God lets loose the terrifying artillery of heaven, His glance is stern toward His enemies, but a tear is in His eye for His people. He is always tender toward them. "Spare My people," He says, and the angels intervene, lest any of His chosen should *"dash* [his] *foot against a stone"* (Psalm 91:12).

People have their treasures—their pearls, their jewels, their rubies, their diamonds—these are their special valuables. Likewise, all who are in the covenant of grace are *"a peculiar treasure"* (Exodus 19:5) of God. He values them above all other beings. In fact, He keeps the world spinning for them. The world exists only to serve as a scaffold for His church. He will send creation packing once His children no longer live on earth. Sun, moon, and stars will pass away like worn-out rags once He has gathered together His own elect and enclosed them forever within the safety of the walls of heaven. Time goes on for the sake of the elect; for them the world exists. He measures the nations according to their number, and He makes the very stars of heaven fight against their enemies and defend them against their foes.

"They shall be to me a people." The favor that is contained in such love cannot be expressed in earthly language. Perhaps on some of those quiet resting places prepared for the saints in heaven, a part of our eternal enjoyment will be to contemplate that love. May we *"be able to comprehend with all saints what is the breadth, and length, and depth,*

and height" (Ephesians 3:18) of these precious, golden thoughts.

THE BENEFICIARIES OF THE COVENANT

Just now, I have a practical consideration to discuss, which is to inquire, For whom has God made this covenant? I have already stated that He made it with Christ, but He made it with Christ as the Representative of His people. Each one of us must answer for himself certain questions, which are: Do I have a personal interest or a share in *"the inheritance of the saints in light"* (Colossians 1:12)? Did Christ Jesus specifically represent me in fulfilling the covenant?

Now, if I were to say that Christ is the Representative of the whole world, you would not find any substantial advantage in that. Since the great proportion of mankind is lost, whatever interest they may have in Christ is certainly of no beneficial value to them as to their eternal salvation.

The question I ask is, Do I have such a special interest in Christ that this covenant holds good toward me, so that I will have, or so that I now have, an enlightened mind and sanctified affections, and so that I possess God as my own God? Be not deceived, my friends, not one of us can turn over the pages of the book of destiny. It is impossible for us to force our way into the council chamber of the Eternal. I hope you are not deluded by superstitious ideas that a special revelation has been given to you, or that you have had some unique dream that makes you think that you are a Christian.

It is on sounder premises that I will try to help you a little. Have you already obtained any of these covenant blessings? Has your mind been enlightened? Do you now find that your spirit tells you what is right and what is wrong? Better still, do you have a love for what is good and a hatred for what is evil (Amos 5:15)? If so, since you have one covenant blessing, all the rest go with it.

Dear one, has your nature undergone a great change? Have you come to hate what you once loved and to love what you once hated? If you have, the covenant lies before you like Canaan before the enraptured eyes of Moses, as he stood on the mountaintop. Look now, for it is yours. It flows with milk and honey, and it belongs to you. You have inherited it.

However, if there has been no such change in you, I cannot hold out any congratulations to you, but I thank God I can do what may serve to bring about this change in your heart. I can hold out divine direction to you; the way to obtain an interest in this covenant and to secure your interest in it is simple. It is contained in just a few words. Pay attention to these three words: "Believe and live." Whoever believes in Christ Jesus has everlasting life, which is the blessing of the covenant. The argument is obvious. Having the blessing of the covenant, you must be in the covenant; and being in the covenant, Christ evidently must have stood as your Representative or Sponsor.

"But," someone asks, "what does it mean to believe in Christ?" There is another word that is a synonym for *believe*—it is *trust*. "How do I know whether Christ died for me in particular?" Trust

Him whether you know that or not. Jesus Christ is lifted up upon the cross of Calvary as the atonement for sin; and the proclamation has been given that everyone who looks upon Him will live (Numbers 21:8). Whoever will cast away his self-righteousness, who will cast away everything upon which he now depends, and who will come and trust in the finished work of our exalted Savior, has in that very faith the indication that he is one of those who were in Christ when He went to the cross and obtained eternal redemption for His elect.

I do not believe that Christ died on the tree to render men salvable, but to save them, really to redeem them. He then and there gave Himself as a ransom. He there paid their debts, there *cast all their sins into the depths of the sea*" (Micah 7:19), and there made a clean sweep of everything that could be laid to the charge of God's elect. You are one of His elect if you believe. Christ died for you if you believe in Him, and your sins are all forgiven.

"But," somebody says, "what about that change of nature that needs to come about?" It always comes with faith. It follows true faith. Wherever there is genuine faith in Christ, faith works in love (Galatians 5:6). A sense of mercy breeds affection; affection for Christ breeds hatred of sin; hatred of sin purges the soul; and, the soul being purged, the life is changed.

The Work of the Covenant of Grace

You must not begin by trying to mend yourself externally. Rather, you must begin with receiving the new internal life, which is found only in this way: *"it is the gift of God"* (Ephesians 2:8) through simply believing in Jesus. That faith in Christ is given to you according to the working of the covenant of grace, for *"it is God which worketh* [faith] *in you"* (Philippians 2:13).

A man who had been for some time attending a certain place of worship had embraced the idea—and a very natural one, too—that he was saved because he had been baptized. He had been to one of those churches where they teach little children to repeat something like this: "In my baptism, wherein I was made a member of Christ, a child of God, and an inheritor of the kingdom of heaven." "Now," said he, very simply and very plainly, according to what that catechism teaches (and a gross delusion it is), "I am saved because I have been baptized; that has made me a child of God."

The good elder who sought to instruct him more soundly and scripturally could find no metaphor that would suit his intellect better than to take a black inkwell and show it to him. "Now," said the mature Christian, "I will wash it." Having washed the outside of that ebony, ink-filled bottle, he invited the man to drink out of it because it was clean. "No," said the man, "it is black, all black; it is not clean just because you have washed the outside." "Oh," came the elder's reply, "and so it is with you; all that those drops of water could do, all that your baptism could do for you, was to wash the outside; but that does not make you clean, for the filth is all within."

The work of the covenant of grace is not to wash the outside, not to cleanse the flesh, not to impose rites and ceremonies and the laying on of hands. Instead, it is to wash the inside, to purge the heart, to cleanse the inner being, to renew the soul. This is the only salvation that will ever enable a man to enter heaven. You may right now renounce all your outward vices, and I hope you will. You may go and practice all of the church rites and ceremonies, and if they are scriptural, I wish you would. However, they will do nothing for you, nothing whatever to enable you to enter heaven, if you miss one other essential thing—that is, obtaining the covenant blessing of the renewed nature, which can only be received as a gift of God through Jesus Christ and as the result of a simple faith in Him who died upon the tree.

I press the work of self-examination upon you. I earnestly urge any church member to apply yourself to this task. It is of no avail that you have joined a religious institution. It is of no avail that you have been baptized. It is of no avail that you take the sacrament of communion. Avail? Indeed, it will bring a greater responsibility and a curse upon you unless your heart has been made new by the Holy Spirit according to the covenant of promise. If you do not have a new heart, go to a quiet place, fall upon your knees, and cry to God for it. May the Holy Spirit constrain you so to do. While you are pleading, remember that the new heart comes from the bleeding heart, and the changed nature comes from the suffering nature. You must look to Jesus, and looking to Jesus, know this:

> There is life in a look at the Crucified One,
> There is life at this moment for thee.

THE BLESSINGS OF THE COVENANT OF GRACE

These blessings of the covenant seem to me to be a great consolation and inspiration. Their comfort comes in different ways to believers everywhere.

A Source of Consolation

The covenant blessings can be a great source of consolation for you. You are in the covenant, my dear friend, but you tell me you are very poor. God has said to you, *"I will be your God"* (Jeremiah 7:23). Why, then, you are very rich! A man may not have a penny to his name, but if he has a diamond, he is rich. Therefore, even though a man may have neither penny nor diamond, if he has his God, he has the *"one pearl of great price"* (Matthew 13:46), and he is rich beyond measure.

Yet, you tell me that your coat is threadbare, and you do not see where you are going to obtain the money to buy a new one.

> [28] *Why take ye thought for raiment? Consider the lilies of the field, how they grow; they toil not, neither do they spin:*
> [29] *And yet I say unto you, That even Solomon in all his glory was not arrayed like one of these.*
> (Matthew 6:28–29)

Remember, you have the same God as the lilies have:

> [30] *Wherefore, if God so clothe the grass of the field, which to day is, and to morrow is cast into the oven, shall he not much more clothe you, O ye of little faith?*

³¹ *Therefore take no thought, saying, What shall we eat? or, What shall we drink? or, Wherewithal shall we be clothed?*
³² *(For after all these things do the Gentiles seek:) for your heavenly Father knoweth that ye have need of all these things.*
³³ *But seek ye first the kingdom of God, and his righteousness; and all these things shall be added unto you.* (Matthew 6:30–33)

Therefore, console yourself with the remembrance of these covenant blessings, but especially that *"my God shall supply all your need according to his riches in glory by Christ Jesus"* (Philippians 4:19).

A Source of Inspiration

I also stated that the covenant of grace should be a great source of inspiration for believers, and I think it is. The covenant is an inspiration for us all to work for Christ, because we are sure to have some results.

² *Therefore said he unto them, The harvest truly is great, but the labourers are few: pray ye therefore the Lord of the harvest, that he would send forth labourers into his harvest.* (Luke 10:2)

³⁵ *Say not ye, There are yet four months, and then cometh harvest? behold, I say unto you, Lift up your eyes, and look on the fields; for they are white already to harvest.*
³⁶ *And he that reapeth receiveth wages, and gathereth fruit unto life eternal: that both he that soweth and he that reapeth may rejoice together.*
(John 4:35–36)

[9] *In due season we shall reap, if we faint not.*
(Galatians 6:9)

I desire, indeed, I desire that the nations would be converted to Christ. I long for all of London to belong to my Lord and Master and every street to be inhabited by those who love His name. Yet, when I see sin abounding and the Gospel often in retreat, I fall back upon this: *"Nevertheless the foundation of God standeth sure, having this seal, The Lord knoweth them that are his"* (2 Timothy 2:19).

Christ will have His own. The infernal powers of hell will not rob our Redeemer. *"He shall see of the travail of his soul, and shall be satisfied"* (Isaiah 53:11). Calvary does not mean defeat. Gethsemane, a defeat? Impossible! The mighty Man who went up to the cross to bleed and die for us, being also the Son of God, did not go down in defeat there, but achieved a victory. *"He shall see his seed, he shall prolong his days, and the pleasure of the LORD shall prosper in his hand"* (Isaiah 53:10).

If some are not saved, others will be. If, being invited, some do not consider themselves worthy to come to the feast, others will be brought in, even the blind and the deaf and the lame, and the supper will be furnished with guests. If they do not come from our great country, *"these shall come from far: and, lo, these from the north and from the west; and these from the land of Sinim"* (Isaiah 49:12). *"Though Israel be not gathered, yet shall* [Christ] *be glorious in the eyes of the LORD"* (Isaiah 49:5), for then the heathen will be gathered unto Him. Then Egypt will yield herself to the Redeemer, and Ethiopia will stretch out her arms to God (Psalm 68:31); the desert nomad will bow the knee, and the far-off stranger will seek Christ.

Oh, no, beloved, the purposes of God are never frustrated; the eternal will of God is not defeated. Christ has died a glorious death, and He will have a full reward for all of His pain.

> [58] *Therefore, my beloved brethren, be ye stedfast, unmoveable, always abounding in the work of the Lord, forasmuch as ye know that your labour is not in vain in the Lord.* (1 Corinthians 15:58)

Chapter 2

God in the Covenant

I will be their God.
—Jeremiah 32:38

What a glorious covenant the second covenant is! Well might it be called *"a better covenant, which was established upon better promises"* (Hebrews 8:6). It is so glorious that the very thought of it is enough to overwhelm our souls when we discern the amazing condescension and infinite love of God in having framed a covenant for such unworthy creatures, for such glorious purposes, with such impartial motives. It is better than the other covenant, the covenant of works, which was originally made with Adam, but which was renewed with Israel, and spelled out in detail for them, when they came out of Egypt. The covenant of grace is far better than the covenant of works, for it is founded upon a better principle.

29

The old covenant was founded on the principle of merit. Essentially, the covenant conditions were these: "Serve God, and you will be rewarded for it; if you walk perfectly in the fear of the Lord, God will deal well with you, and all the blessings of Mount Gerizim (Deuteronomy 11:29, 27:12) will come upon you, and you will be exceedingly blessed in this world and in the world that is to come." However, the old covenant fell by the wayside. Although it was just that man should be rewarded for his good works or punished for his evil ones, yet the covenant of works was not suitable for man's happiness, nor could it promote his eternal welfare, since man was sure to sin and invariably tended toward iniquity since the Fall.

However, the new covenant is not founded on works at all. It is a covenant of pure, unmingled grace. You may read it from its first word to its last, but you will not find a solitary syllable as to anything to be done by us. The whole covenant is a covenant, not so much between man and his Maker, as it is between the Almighty and man's Representative, the Lord Jesus Christ. The human side of the covenant has been already fulfilled by Jesus, and there remains nothing now but the covenant of giving. The requirements as to the human part of the covenant no longer exist.

The entire covenant of grace, in regard to us as the people of God, now stands this way: "I, your Lord, will give this; I will bestow that; I will fulfill this promise; I will grant that favor." We have to do nothing to merit this grace, for there is nothing we can do. God will work all our works in us, and the very graces that are sometimes represented as being stipulations of the covenant are promised to us. He gives us faith (Ephesians 2:8). He promises to give us the law in our *"inward parts"* and to *"write it on* [our] *hearts"* (Jeremiah 31:33).

It is a glorious covenant, because it is founded on simple mercy and absolutely pure grace. It stands, quite irrespective of any past actions on our part or anything that could yet be performed by man. Hence, this covenant surpasses the other in stability. Where there is anything of man, there is always a degree of inconstancy. Anywhere you have anything to do with created beings, there you have something to do with change, for created beings and change and uncertainty always go together. But, since this new covenant now has nothing whatever to do with mankind—in the sense that mankind does not have to do anything except receive—the idea of change is utterly and entirely gone.

It is God's covenant, and therefore it is an unchanging covenant. If there is something that I am to do in the covenant, then I have no security in the covenant. However, if the covenant is dependent only on God's works, then as long as my name is in that covenant, my soul is as secure as if I were now walking the streets of gold in heaven (Revelation 21:21). If any blessing is in the covenant, I am as certain to receive that blessing as if I had already grasped it in my hands, because the promise of God is sure to be followed by fulfillment. The promise never fails; it always brings with it everything that it is intended to convey. The moment I receive it by faith, I am sure of the blessing itself. How infinitely superior is this covenant to the other in its manifest security! It is beyond the risk or hazard of the least uncertainty.

I have been thinking for the last two or three days that the covenant of grace excels the other covenant most marvelously in the mighty blessings that it confers. What does the covenant of grace convey? Earlier, I even considered entitling this chapter, "The Blessings That the Covenant of Grace Gives to God's Children." Yet, when I began to think of it, I realized that there is so much in the covenant that if I only made a catalog of all of the great and glorious blessings wrapped up within its folds, I would need to occupy nearly an entire library in making a few simple observations about each one.

Consider the great things God has given in the covenant. He sums them up by saying He has *"given unto us all things that pertain unto life and godliness"* (2 Peter 1:3). He has given you eternal life in Christ Jesus; yes, He has given Christ Jesus to be yours. He has made Christ *"heir of all things"* (Hebrews 1:2), and He has made you one of His *"joint-heirs with Christ"* (Romans 8:17). Hence, He has given you everything.

Were I to sum up the vast amount of unutterable treasure that God has conveyed to every elect soul through this glorious covenant, space would fail me. Therefore, I will commence with the greatest benefit conveyed to us by the covenant. This singular blessing is enough to startle us by its immense value. In fact, unless it had been written in God's Word, we never could have dreamed that such a blessing could be ours. By the terms of the covenant,

God Himself becomes the believer's own portion and inheritance: *"I will be their God."*

I will begin with the subject in this way. I will show you first that this is a special blessing: *"I will be their God."* God is the special possession of the elect, whose names are in the covenant. Secondly, I will discuss this as being an exceedingly precious blessing: *"I will be their God."* Thirdly, I will dwell upon the security of this blessing: *"I will be their God."* Then, I will endeavor to encourage you to make good use of this blessing, which has been so freely and liberally conveyed to you by the eternal covenant of grace: *"I will be their God."*

Stop a moment, and think about this promise before we go on. In the covenant of grace, God conveys Himself to you and becomes yours. May you comprehend this truth and take it personally to heart. All that is meant by the word *GOD*: eternity, infinity, omnipotence, omniscience, perfect justice, infallible integrity, eternal love; all that is meant by *GOD*: Creator, Guardian, Preserver, Governor, Judge; all that the word *GOD* can mean: all of goodness and of love, all of bounty and of grace—all that and more this covenant gives you to be your absolute property as much as anything you can call your own. *"I will be their God."* Reflect on that thought. If this truth is opened up and applied by the all-glorious Spirit to your heart and life, there is enough in it to excite your joy for all eternity: *"I will be their God."*

> My God! How cheerful is the sound!
> How pleasant to repeat!
> Well may that heart with pleasure bound,
> Where God hath fixed His seat.

THE UNIVERSAL POWERS OF GOD

How is God especially the God of His own children? God is the God of all men, of all creatures; He is the God of the lowly worm, of the flying eagle, of the bright star, and of the billowy cloud; He is God everywhere. How then is He more my God and your God than He is the God of all created things? In some ways God is the God of all His creatures, but even in these ways a special relationship exists between Himself and His chosen ones, whom He has loved *"with an everlasting love"* (Jeremiah 31:3). In addition, there are certain ways of relating that do not exist between God and His creatures, except with His own children.

As Sovereign

First, God is the God of all His creatures in that He has the sovereign right to deal with them as He pleases. He is the Creator of all; as such, He is the supreme Sovereign of the universe. He is the Potter and has *"power over the clay, of the same lump to make one vessel unto honour, and another unto dishonour"* (Romans 9:21). However men may sin against God, He is still their God in the sense that their destinies are immovably in His hand. He can do with them exactly as He chooses. However they may resent His will or spurn His good pleasure, yet He makes the wrath of man to praise Him, and the remainder of that wrath He restrains (Psalm 76:10). He is the God of all creatures, and absolutely so in the matter of predestination, seeing that He is their

Creator and has an absolute right to do with them as
He wills.

However, God the Father has a special regard
for His children. He is their God in this way: while
He exercises the same sovereignty over them, He
exercises it in grace and grace only. He makes them
the vessels of His mercy, who will be to His honor
forever. He has chosen them out of the ruins of the
Fall and has made them heirs of everlasting life,
while He allows the rest of the world to continue in
sin and to fulfill their guilt by well-deserved punishment. Thus, while His relationship with all His
creatures is the same as far as His sovereignty and
His right of determination are concerned, there is
something special in the aspect of His love toward
His people. In this sense, He is their God.

As Governor

Further, He is the God of all His creatures in
that He has a right to command obedience of all. He
is the God of every person who was ever born into
this earth, because everyone is bound to obey Him.
God can command the homage of all of His creatures
because He is their Creator, Governor, and Preserver. All men are, by the fact of their creation, so
placed in subjection to Him that they cannot escape
the obligation of submission to His laws.

Even in this aspect, however, there is something
special regarding His relationship with His child.
Although God is the Ruler of all men, yet His rule is
special toward His children. He lays aside the sword
of His rulership; in His hand He grasps the rod of

correction for His child, not the sword of punitive vengeance. While He gives the world a law written on stone, He gives to His children laws written in their hearts (Jeremiah 31:33).

God is my Governor and yours, but if you are unregenerate, He is your Governor in a different sense than He is mine. He has ten times as much claim to my obedience as He has to yours. Seeing that He has done more for me, I am bound to do more for Him. Seeing that He has loved me more, I am bound to love Him more. However, should I disobey, the vengeance on my head will not fall as heavily as it would on yours, if you are outside of Christ. The vengeance incurred by me has already fallen upon Christ, my Substitute, and only the chastisement will remain for me. Here again, we see that while God's relationship to all men is universal, there is something special in it in reference to His children.

As Judge

Next, God has a universal power over all His creatures in His office of Judge. *"With righteousness shall he judge the world, and the people with equity"* (Psalm 98:9). It is true that He will judge all men with righteousness. However, as if His people were *"not of the world"* (John 15:19), the additional statement is added, *"and* [His] *people with equity."* God is the God of all creatures, I repeat, in the sense that He is their Judge. He will summon them all before His bar to condemn or acquit each and every one of them.

However, even at the judgment seat, there is something exceptional regarding His children, for to them the condemnation sentence will never come, only the acquittal. While He is Judge of all, He especially is their Judge. He is the Judge whom they love to reverence, the Judge whom they long to approach, because they know His lips will confirm that which their hearts have already felt—the sentence of their full acquittal through the merits of their glorious Savior. Our loving God is the Judge who will acquit our souls, and in that respect we can say He is our God.

So then, whether as Sovereign in determining outcomes, as Governor in enforcing the law, or as Judge in punishing sin, God is the God of all men. Yet, in each of these aspects of God's divine character, there is something special in the way He relates to His people, so that they can say, "He is our God, even in these relationships."

OUR GOD IN SPECIAL WAYS

But now, beloved, there are other aspects of the way God relates to His children that the rest of His creatures cannot benefit from, and here the great crux of the matter lies. Here the very heart of this glorious promise dwells. God is our God in a sense that the unregenerate, the unconverted, the unholy, can never know, and in a way in which they have no part whatever. We have just considered other points with regard to what God is to man generally. Let us now consider what He is to His children, as He is to no one else.

In Election

First of all, God is my God in that He is the God of my election. If I am His child, then He loved me from before the creation of the universe, and His infinite mind made plans for my salvation long before He ever framed the worlds by His word (Hebrews 11:3):

> ⁴ *According as he hath chosen us in him before the foundation of the world, that we should be holy and without blame before him in love:*
> ⁵ *Having predestinated us unto the adoption of children by Jesus Christ to himself, according to the good pleasure of his will.* (Ephesians 1:4–5)

If He is my God, He has seen me when I have wandered far from Him. When I have rebelled, His mind has determined when my path would be blocked and I would be turned from the error of my ways. He has been providing for me the means of grace. He has applied those means of grace in due time, but His everlasting purpose has been the basis and the foundation of it all. Thus, He is my God as He is the God of no one else besides His own children. He is my glorious, gracious God in eternal election, for He thought of me and chose me from *"before the foundation of the world, that* [I] *should be holy and without blame before him in love."*

Looking back, then, I see election's God, and election's God is my God if I am in election. However, if I do not fear God or even have any thoughts of Him, then He is another man's God and not mine. If I have no claim and participation in election, then I am compelled to look upon Him as being the God of a great body of people whom He has chosen, but not my God. If I can look back and see my name *"written in the Lamb's book of life"* (Revelation 21:27), then indeed He is my God in election.

In Justification

Furthermore, the Christian can call God his God from the fact of his justification. A sinner can call God, "God," but he must always put in an adjective and speak of God as an angry God, an incensed God, or an offended God. In contrast, the Christian can say, "my God," without putting in any adjective except a sweet one with which to extol Him, for now we *"who sometimes were far off are made nigh by the blood of Christ"* (Ephesians 2:13). We who were enemies of God because of our wicked states are now His friends. Looking up to Him, I can say, "my God," for He is my Friend, and I am His friend. Enoch could say, "my God," because he walked with Him (Genesis 5:24). Adam could not say, "my God," when he hid himself in the Garden after he had sinned. So, while I, as a sinner, run from God, I cannot call Him mine; but when I have peace with God and am brought near to Him, then indeed He is my God and my Friend.

By Adoption

God the Father is also the believer's God by adoption, and in that the sinner has no part. I have heard people represent God as the Father of the whole universe. It surprises me that any reader of

the Bible would talk like that. Paul once quoted a
heathen poet, who said that *"we are also his off-
spring"* (Acts 17:28); and it is true in some sense
that we are, as having been created by Him. But in
the high sense in which the term *children* is used in
Scripture to express the holy relationship of a regenerate child toward his Father, none can say, "my Father," except those who have *"Abba, Father"* (Romans
8:15) imprinted on their hearts by the Spirit of
Adoption. By the Holy Spirit, God becomes my God
in a way in which He is not the God of others. The
Christian has a special claim to God, because God is
his Father in ways He is not the Father of anyone
except a person who is His child.

Beloved, these things are quite enough to show
you that in special ways God is the God of His own
people. I must leave this to your own meditations,
which will suggest twenty different ways in which
God is specially the God of His own children more
than He is of the rest of His creatures. "God," say
the wicked, but "my God," say God's children.

As Covering

Then, if God is your God personally, let Him
clothe and cover you according to your position as
His child. Be adorned with *"the Sun of righteousness"* (Malachi 4:2). *"Put ye on the Lord Jesus
Christ"* (Romans 13:14). *"The king's daughter is"*—
and so let all the King's sons be—*"all glorious
within: her clothing is of wrought gold"* (Psalm
45:13). *"Be clothed with humility"* (1 Peter 5:5). Put
on love, compassion, gentleness, and meekness; and

say as you do so, *"He hath clothed me with the garments of salvation, he hath covered me with the robe of righteousness"* (Isaiah 61:10).

Let your company and conversation be according to your clothing. Live among the excellent, among the generation of the just; go *"to the general assembly and church of the firstborn...and to the spirits of just men made perfect"* (Hebrews 12:23). Live in the courts of the great King. Behold His face, wait at His throne, bear His name, show forth His virtues, set forth His praises, advance His honor, uphold His interests. Let vile persons and vile ways be condemned in your eyes; be of a more noble spirit than to be companions with them. Regard not their associations or their scorns, their flatteries or their frowns. Rejoice not with their joys, fear not their fears, care not their cares, eat not their dainties. Go out from among them to your country, your city, where no unclean thing can enter or annoy. Live by faith, in the power of the Spirit, in the beauty of holiness, in the hope of the Gospel, in the joy of your God, in the magnificence and the humility of the children of the great King.

EXCEEDINGLY PRECIOUS GRACE

Now, for a moment, let us consider the exceeding preciousness of this great mercy: *"I will be their God."* I imagine that God Himself could say no more than that. I do not believe if the Infinite were to stretch His powers and magnify His grace by some stupendous promise that could outdo every other, that it could exceed in glory this promise: *"I will be their God."* Oh, Christian, do consider what it is to have God as your own! Consider what it is, especially in comparison with anything else.

> Jacob's portion is the Lord;
>> What can Jacob more require?
> What can heaven more afford,
>> Or a creature more desire?

Compare your life with the lot of your fellow-men. Some of them have their portion in the fields; they are *"rich, and increased with goods, and have need of nothing"* (Revelation 3:17); their yellow harvests are even now ripening in the sun. But what are harvests compared with your God, the Lord of the Harvest? Or, what are full granaries compared with God who is your Husbandman (John 15:1) and feeds you with *"the true bread from heaven"* (John 6:32)?

Some have their portion in the city; their wealth is superabundant; it flows to them in constant streams, until they become a very reservoir of gold. But what is gold compared with your God? You could not live on it; your spiritual life could not be sustained by it. If you applied it to your aching head, would it afford you any ease? If you put it on a troubled conscience, would your gold assuage its pangs? If you put it on your despondent heart, would it soothe even one solitary groan or give you one less grief? But you have God, and in Him you have more than gold or riches could ever buy, more than heaps of brilliant ore could ever purchase for you.

Some have their portion in this world, in what most men love, applause and fame. Yet, ask yourself, is not your God more to you than that? If a thousand

trumpets would proclaim your praise, and if a myr-
iad cornets would loudly resound with ovations for
you, what would it all mean to you if you had lost
your God? Would this calm the turmoil of your soul
that is ill at ease with itself? Would this prepare you
to pass through the Jordan and to encounter those
stormy waves that finally must be forded by every
man, when he is called from this world to lands beyond? Would a puff of wind serve you then, or would
the clapping of the hands of your fellow creatures
bless you on your deathbed? No, there are griefs here
with which men cannot meddle, and there are griefs
to come with which men cannot interfere to alleviate
the pangs and pains and agonies and dying strife.

However, when you have this—*"I will be your
God"* (Jeremiah 11:4)—you have as much as all
other men can have put together, for earthly things
are all they have. How little ought we to estimate
the value of the treasures of this world, especially
when we consider that God frequently gives the
most riches to the worst of His creatures! As Martin
Luther said, "God gives food to His children and
husks to His swine; and who are the swine that get
the husks?" It is not often that God's people get the
riches of this world; this only proves that material
riches are of little real worth, or else God would give
them to us. Abraham gave the sons of Keturah
"gifts, and sent them away" (Genesis 25:6). Let me
be Isaac and have my Father in heaven, and the
world may take all the rest. Oh, Christian, ask for
nothing in this world, except that you may live and
die on this: *"I will be their God."* This exceeds all the
world has to offer.

Compare this with what you need, Christian. What do you require? Is there not here all that you need? To make you happy, you want something that will satisfy you. Come now, is not this enough? Will not this fill your pitcher to its very brim, until it runs over? If you can put this promise inside your cup, will you not be forced to say, with David, "*'My cup runneth over'* (Psalm 23:5); I have more than any heart can wish"? When this is fulfilled, when the Lord says to you, *"I am your God"* (Ezekiel 34:31), let your cup be completely empty of earthly things.

Suppose you have not one solitary drop of earthly happiness, yet is not His promise enough to fill your cup until your unsteady hand cannot hold it because of its fullness? Are you not complete when God is yours? Do you want anything except God? If you think you do, it would be good for you to remain without it, for all you want, apart from God, is only to gratify your lust. Christian, is not the fact that God is your God enough to satisfy you, even if all else should fail?

However, you want more than quiet satisfaction. Sometimes you desire rapturous delight. Come, soul, is there not enough here to delight you? Put this promise to your lips. Did you ever drink wine half as sweet as this: *"I will be their God"*? Did trumpet or harp ever sound half as sweet as this: *"I will be their God"*? Not all the music blown from harmonious instruments or drawn from living strings could ever give such melody as this sweet promise: *"I will be their God."* Oh, here is a sea of bliss, an ocean of delight. Come, bathe your spirit in it; you may swim to eternity and never find a shore. You may dive to the very infinite depths and never find the bottom. *"I will be their God."* If this does not make your eyes sparkle, if this does not make your feet dance for joy and your heart soar with bliss, then assuredly your soul is not in a healthy state.

However, you want something more than present delights. You desire something concerning which you may exercise hope. What more could you ever hope to get than the fulfillment of this great promise: *"I will be their God"*? Oh, hope, you are a great-handed thing; you lay hold of mighty things that even faith does not have the power to grasp. Yet, although your hand may be very large, this blessing fills it, so that you can carry nothing else.

I declare before God that I have not a hope beyond this promise: *"I will be their God."* "Oh," you say, "you have a hope of heaven." Yes, I have a hope of heaven, but this is heaven: *"I will be their God."* What is heaven, but to be with God, to dwell with Him, to realize that God is mine and I am His? I say I have not a hope beyond that. There is not a promise beyond that, for all promises rest on this, and all hopes are included in this: *"I will be their God."*

"I will be their God" is the masterpiece of all promises. It is the capstone of all the great and precious things that God has provided for His children. If we could really grasp it, if it could be applied to our souls so that we could understand it, we might clap our hands and say, "Oh, the wonder! Oh, the glory! Oh, the graciousness of that promise!" It makes a heaven below, and it must make a heaven above. Nothing else will ever truly be needed except this: *"I will be their God."*

THE CERTAINTY OF THE PROMISE

Now, let us briefly consider the certainty of this promise. It does not say, "I may be their God," but, *"I will be their God."* Nor does the text say, "Perhaps I will be their God." No, it says, *"I will be their God."*

Let us suppose there is a sinner who says he will not have God for his God. He will have God to be His preserver, to take care of him and keep him from harm. He does not object to God feeding him, giving him his bread and water and clothing. Nor does he mind making God somewhat of a showpiece that he may take out on Sundays and bow before. However, he will not have God for his God; he will not take Him to be his all. He makes his belly his god (Philippians 3:19), gold his god, the world his god. How is God's promise to be fulfilled in this sinner?

Here is one of God's chosen people, but he does not know that he is chosen yet, and he says he will not have God. How then is this promise to be carried out? "Oh," say some, "if the man won't have God, then, of course, God cannot win him." We have heard it preached, and we read it frequently, that salvation entirely depends upon man's will: that if man stands back and resists God's Holy Spirit, the creature can be the conqueror of the Creator, and finite power can overcome the Infinite.

Frequently, I take up a book and read this: "Sinner, be willing, for unless you are, God cannot save you." Sometimes the question is asked: "How is it that a certain person is not saved?" Often, the answer is given: "He is not willing to be; God strove with him, but he would not be saved." But, suppose God had striven with him as He has done with those who are saved. Would he have been saved then? The usual reply is this: "No, he would have resisted." Instead, I answer, "It is not dependent on man's will; it is '*not of blood, nor of the will of the flesh, nor of the will of man, but of God*'" (John 1:13). We should never entertain such absurd ideas as the notion that man can conquer Omnipotence or the thought that the might of man is greater than God's might.

I believe, indeed, that certain usual influences of the Holy Spirit may be withstood. I believe that there are general operations of the Spirit in many men's hearts that are resisted and rejected. However, I believe that the effectual working of the Holy Spirit, with the determination to save, cannot be resisted, unless you suppose that God can be overcome by His creatures and that the purpose of Deity can be frustrated by the will of man, which would be to suppose something akin to blasphemy.

Beloved, God has power to fulfill the promise, "*I will be their God.*"

The sinner cries, "I will not have You for a God."

"Is that so?" says He, and He gives him over to the hand of Moses. Moses takes the person for a little while and applies the club of the law, dragging him to Sinai, where the mountain towers over his head as lightning flashes and thunder bellows.

Then the sinner cries, "O God, save me!"

"I thought you would not have me for a God," He replies.

"O Lord, You shall be my God," says the poor, trembling sinner. "I have stripped myself of all my ornaments (Exodus 33:6). O Lord, what will you do to me? Save me! I give myself to You. Oh, take me!"

"Yes," says the Lord, "I knew it. I said that *'I will be their God,'* and I have made you *'willing in the day of* [My] *power'"* (Psalm 110:3). *"I will be their God, and they shall be my people"* (Ezekiel 37:27).

MAKING USE OF THIS BLESSING

Now, lastly, I urge you to make use of God, if He is yours. It is strange that spiritual blessings are our only possessions that we do not use. We get a great spiritual blessing, and we let it rust away for many a day. There is the mercy seat, for instance. My friends, if you had a cash box as full of riches as that mercy seat is, you would go often to it, as often as your necessities require. Yet, you do not go to the mercy seat half as often as you need to go. Most of the precious things God has given to us we never overuse. The truth is, they cannot be overused. We cannot wear a promise threadbare. We can never burn out the incense of grace. We can never use up the infinite treasures of God's lovingkindness.

If the blessings God gives us are not used, perhaps God Himself is the least used of all. Although He is our God, we turn to and seek Him less than we turn to any of our kindred human beings or seek any of His mercies that He bestows upon us.

Look at the example of the poor heathen; they use their gods, although they are no gods. They put up a piece of wood or stone and call it God. And how they use it! They want rain: the people assemble and ask for rain in the firm but foolish hope that their god can give it. There is a battle, and their god is lifted up. He is brought out from the house where he usually dwells, so that he may go before them and lead them on to victory.

Receive Guidance

Yet, how seldom God's children ask counsel at the hands of the Lord! How often we go about our business without asking His guidance! In our troubles, do we not constantly strive to bear our burdens, instead of casting them upon the Lord, in order that He may sustain us? This is not because we may not, for the Lord says, *"'Come unto me, all ye that labour and are heavy laden, and I will give you rest'* (Matthew 11:28). I am yours, My child; come and make use of Me as you will. You may freely come to My storehouse, and the more often, the better. Welcome." Have you set God in the background, having no purpose in your life? Do not let your God be as other gods, serving only for show. Do not let your relationship with God be in name only. Since He allows you, and since you have such a Friend, use Him daily for caring, wise guidance.

Have Your Needs Met

"My God shall supply all your need according to his riches in glory by Christ Jesus" (Philippians 4:19). Never lack anything while you have God; never fear or faint while you have God. Go to your treasure chest, and take whatever you need. There

you will find bread and clothing and health and life and all that you need. Beloved, learn the divine skill of making God all things; learn to make bread of your God, and water and health and friends and ease. He can supply you with all of these. Better still, He can be your food, your clothing, your friend, your life. All this He said to you in this promise: *"I am your God"* (Ezekiel 34:31).

Find Companionship

From here on, you may say, as a heaven-born saint once did, "I have no husband, and yet I am no widow, for my Maker is my husband (Isaiah 54:5). I have no father or friend, and yet I am neither fatherless (Psalm 68:5) nor friendless; my God is both my Father and my Friend. I have no child, but He is better to me than ten children (1 Samuel 1:8). I have no house, but yet I have a home; I have made the Most High my habitation (Psalm 91:9). I am alone, yet I am not by myself, for my Father has not left me alone (John 8:29) and is good company for me. With Him I can walk; with Him I can take sweet counsel and sweet repose. When I go to bed, when I arise, while I am in my house, and as I conduct my daily business, my God is always with me (Matthew 28:20). With Him I travel, I dwell, I lodge, I live, and I will live forever."

Be Comforted in Prayer

Oh, child of God, let me urge you to make use of your God. Make use of Him in prayer. I implore you to go to Him often, because He is your God. If He were another man's God, you might weary Him; but He is your God. If He were my God and not yours, you would have no right to approach Him. However, He is your God. He has "made Himself over" to you like a bank check, if I may use such an expression. He has become the incontestable property of all His children, so that all He has and all He is, is theirs. O child, will you let your treasury lie idle, when you need it? No, go and draw from it by prayer.

Run to Him in Times of Trouble

To Him in every trouble flee,
Thy best, thy only, Friend.

Run to Him. Tell Him all your needs. Use Him constantly by faith, at all times. I plead with you, if some dark cloud has come over you, use your God as a sun, for He is *"the Sun of righteousness"* (Malachi 4:2). If some strong enemy has come against you, use your God for a shield, for He is a shield to protect you (Psalm 3:3). If you have lost your way in the maze of life, use Him as your guide, for the great Jehovah will direct you. If you are in the midst of storms, use Him as your pilot, for He is the God who stills the raging of the sea and says unto the waves, *"Peace, be still"* (Mark 4:39). If you are a poor thing, not knowing which way to turn, use Him for your shepherd; remind yourself that *"the LORD is my shepherd; I shall not want"* (Psalm 23:1). Whatever you are, wherever you are, remember that God is just what you need, and He is just where you need Him to be.

51

I urge you to make use of your God for all your wants and needs. Do not forget Him in your trouble, but flee to Him in the midst of your distresses, crying,

> When all created streams are dried,
> Your fullness is the same;
> May I with this be satisfied,
> And glory in Thy name!
>
> No good in creatures can be found,
> But may be found in Thee.
> I must have all things, and abound,
> While God is God to me.

Take Delight in Your God

Beloved, let me persuade you to allow God to be your delight this day. If you have trials, or if you are free from them, I urge you, make God your delight. Be happy right now in the Lord. Remember, it is a commandment: *"Rejoice in the Lord alway: and again I say, Rejoice"* (Philippians 4:4). Do not be content to be moderately happy; seek to soar to the heights of bliss and to enjoy a heaven below. Get near to God, and you will get near to heaven. It is not as it is here on earth where the higher you go, the colder you find it, because on the mountain there is nothing to reflect the rays of the sun. Instead, with God, the nearer you go to Him, the brighter He will shine upon you, and the warmer you will be. When there are no other creatures to reflect His goodness, His light will be all the brighter. Go to God continually, persistently, confidently.

[4] *Delight thyself also in the LORD; and he shall give thee the desires of thine heart.*

[5] *Commit thy way unto the LORD; trust also in him; and he shall bring it to pass.*   (Psalm 37:4–5)

[24] *Thou shalt guide me with thy counsel, and afterward receive me to glory.*   (Psalm 73:24)

"I will be their God" is the first blessing of the covenant; the second is equal to it. We will consider that in the next chapter.

Chapter 3

Christ in the Covenant

I will...give thee for a covenant of the people.
—Isaiah 49:8

We all believe that our Savior has very much to do with the covenant of eternal salvation. We have learned to regard Him as the Mediator of the covenant, as the Surety of the covenant, and as the Substance of the covenant.

We consider Him to be the Mediator of the covenant, for we are certain that God could make no covenant with man unless there were a mediator, a middleman who could stand between them both. We hail Him as the Mediator, who, with mercy in His hands, came down to tell sinful man the good news that grace was promised in the eternal counsel of the Most High.

We also love our Savior as the Surety of the covenant. On our behalf, He undertook to pay our debts. On His Father's behalf, He also undertook to see that all of the souls of His elect would be secure and safe, and that every one of the Father's children would ultimately be presented unblemished and complete before Him.

Moreover, I do not doubt that we also rejoice in the thought that Christ is the Substance of the covenant. We believe that when we sum up all spiritual blessings, we must say, *"Christ is all, and in all"* (Colossians 3:11). He is the matter, He is the essence, of it. Although much might be said concerning the glories of the covenant, yet nothing could be said that is not to be found in that one word *Christ.*

However, at this time I will dwell on Christ, not as the Mediator, nor as the Surety, nor as the Substance of the covenant, but as the one great and glorious Bequest of the covenant that God has given to His children. It is our firm belief that Christ is ours and has been given to us by God. We know *"that* [God] *spared not his own Son, but delivered him up for us all,"* and we therefore believe that He will *"with him freely give us all things"* (Romans 8:32). We can say, with the spouse, *"My beloved is mine, and I am his"* (Song 2:16). We feel that we have a personal share in our Lord and Savior Jesus Christ. It will therefore delight us, in the best manner possible, without the garnishment of eloquence or the trappings of flowery rhetoric, just to meditate upon this great thought: in the covenant Jesus Christ is the portion of every believer.

First, we will undertake to examine this bestowed inheritance. Secondly, we will notice the purpose for which it was conveyed to us. And then, we will explore one principle of relationship with Christ that may well be affixed to such a great blessing as this, and is indeed an inference from it.

THE BELIEVER'S GREAT INHERITANCE

First, here is every Christian's great possession: Jesus Christ is the portion of each believer by the terms of the covenant. By this, we must understand Jesus Christ in many different senses.

We will begin, first of all, by declaring that Jesus Christ is ours in all His attributes. He has a double set of attributes, seeing that there are two natures joined in glorious union in one Person. He has the attributes of very God, and He has the attributes of perfect Man. Whatever these may be, they are each one of them the perpetual property of every believing child of God.

In All of His Attributes As God

I do not need to dwell on Christ's attributes as God. You already know how infinite His love is, how vast His grace, how firm His faithfulness, how unswerving His veracity! You know that He is omniscient, you know that He is omnipresent, and you know that He is omnipotent.

It would be a great consolation to you if you could realize that all these great and glorious attributes that belong to God are yours. Does He have power? His power is yours—yours to support and strengthen you, yours to overcome your enemies, yours to keep you firmly secure. Does He have love? There is not a particle of love in His great heart that is not yours; all His love belongs to you. You may dive into the immense, bottomless ocean of His love, and you may say of it all, "It is mine." Does He have justice? This may seem a stern attribute, but even that is yours; by His justice He will see to it that all that is covenanted to you by the oath and promise of God will be most certainly granted to you. Believer, mention whatever you please that is a characteristic of Christ as the ever glorious Son of God, and you may put your hand upon it and say, "It is mine."

Your arm, O Jesus, upon which the pillars of the earth do hang, is mine. Those eyes, O Jesus, which pierce through the thick darkness and behold the future—Your eyes are mine, to look on me with love. Those lips, O Christ, which sometimes speak words louder than ten thousand thunders or whisper syllables sweeter than the music of the harps of the glorified—those lips are mine. And that heart, which beats high with such unselfish, pure, and genuine love—that heart is mine. The whole of You, in all Your glorious nature as the Son of God, as God over all, blessed forever, is mine—positively, actually, without metaphor, in reality mine.

In All of His Attributes As Man

Consider Him as a man, too. All that He has as perfect Man is yours. As perfect Man, He stood before His Father, *full of grace and truth*" (John 1:14), full of favor, and accepted by God as a perfect being. O believer, God's acceptance of Christ is your acceptance. Do you not know that the same love that the Father set on a perfect Christ, He now sets on you? All that Christ did is Yours. The perfect righteousness that Jesus lived out, when through His stainless life He kept the law and made it honorable, is yours. There is not a virtue Christ ever had that is not yours; there is not a holy deed He ever did that is not yours. There is not a prayer He ever sent to heaven that is not yours. There is not one solitary thought toward God, which it was His duty to think and which He thought as a man serving His God, that is not yours. All His righteousness, in its vast extent and in all the perfection of His character, is imputed to you.

Oh, believer, think of all that you have obtained in the word *Christ*. Come, consider that word *God*, and think how mighty it is. Then meditate upon the idea of the perfect man: all that Christ, as the man-God and the glorious God-man, ever had or ever can have, as the characteristic of either of His natures, is yours. It all belongs to you. It is given out of pure, free favor and is beyond the fear of revocation, passed on to you to be your actual property— and that forever.

In All of His Offices

Then, consider, believer, that not only is Christ yours in all His attributes, but He is yours in all His offices. Great and glorious these offices are; I scarcely have space to mention them all. Is He a prophet? Then He is your Prophet. Is He a priest? Then He is your Priest. Is He a king? Then He is your King. Is He a redeemer? Then He is your Redeemer. Is He an advocate? Then He is your Advocate. Is He a forerunner? Then He is your Forerunner. Is He a surety of the covenant? Then He is your Surety. In every name He bears, in every crown He wears, in every vestment in which He is arrayed, Christ is the believer's own.

Child of God, if you had grace to gather up this thought into your soul, it would comfort you marvelously to think that in all Christ is in His offices, He is most assuredly yours. Do you see Him there, interceding before His Father, with outstretched arms? Do you see His ephod and His golden crown on His brow, inscribed with *"HOLINESS TO THE LORD"* (Exodus 39:30)? Do you see Him as He lifts up His hands to pray? Do you hear His marvelous intercession such as man never prayed on earth, that authoritative intercession such as He Himself could not use in the agonies of the Garden of Gethsemane?

> With sighs and groans, He offered up
> His humble suit below.
> But with authority He pleads,
> Enthroned in glory now.

Do you see how He asks and how He receives, as soon as His petition is lifted up? Can you, dare you, believe that His intercession is all your own, that on His heart your name is engraved, that in His heart your name is stamped in marks of indelible grace, that all the majesty of His surpassing intercession is yours, and that it would all be expended for you if you needed it? Can you comprehend that He has no authority with His Father that He will not use on your behalf, if you require it, and that He has no power to intercede that He would not employ for you in all times of necessity? Come now, words cannot set this forth—it is only your meditations that can teach you this. It is only God the Holy Spirit bringing home the truth that can set this rapturous, transporting thought in its proper position in your heart: that Christ is yours in all He is and has.

Do you see Him on earth? There He stands, the Great High Priest, offering His bloody sacrifice. See Him on the tree: His hands are pierced, His blood gushes forth from His wounds. Oh! Do you see that pale countenance and those languid eyes filled with compassion? Do you observe that crown of thorns? Do you behold that mightiest of sacrifices, the sum and substance of them all? Believer, all that is yours: those precious drops plead and claim your peace with God; that open side is your refuge; those pierced hands are your redemption; that groan, He groans for you; that cry of a forsaken heart, He utters for you; that death, He died for you.

Come, I urge you to consider Christ in any one of His various offices. However, when you do consider Him, lay hold of this thought: in all these things He is your Christ, given unto you in the eternal covenant as your possession forever.

In All of His Works

Notice next that Christ is the believer's in every one of His works. Whether they are works of suffering or of duty, they are the property of the believer. As an infant, He was circumcised, and is that bloody rite ours? Yes, *"in whom also* [we] *are circumcised with the circumcision made without hands, in putting off the body of the sins of the flesh by the circumcision of Christ"* (Colossians 2:11). As an adult, He was baptized, and is that spiritual sign of watery baptism ours? Yes, we are *"buried with him by baptism into death"* (Romans 6:4). We share Jesus' baptism when we lie interred with our Best Friend in the same watery tomb. See, there He dies, but is His death ours? Yes, we are *"dead with Christ"* (v. 8). He is buried, and is that burial ours? Yes, we are buried with Christ. He rises. See Him startling the guards and rising from the tomb! And is that resurrection ours? Yes, we *"are risen with him through the faith of the operation of God, who hath raised him from the dead"* (Colossians 2:12).

Notice this also: *"When he ascended up on high, he led captivity captive"* (Ephesians 4:8). Is that ascension ours as believers? Yes, for He has *"raised us up together"* (Ephesians 2:6). And see, He sits on His Father's throne; is that place ours? Yes, He has made us to *"sit together in heavenly places"* (v. 6).

All Christ did is ours. By divine decree, there exists such a union between Christ and His people that all Christ did, His people did. All Christ has performed, His people performed in Him, for they were in His loins when He lay in the tomb, and in His loins they have *"ascended up on high"* (v. 8). With Him they entered into bliss, and with Him they sit in heavenly places. Represented by Him, their Head, all His people even now are glorified in Him—even in Him who is *"the head over all things to the church"* (Ephesians 1:22). Remember, believer, that you have a covenant interest in all the deeds of Christ, either in His humiliation or His exaltation, and that all those acts are yours.

In All the Fullness of the Godhead

I would for one moment hint at a sweet thought, which is this: you know that in the person of Christ *"dwelleth all the fulness of the Godhead bodily"* (Colossians 2:9). Now, remember that the Scripture says, *"And of his fulness have all we received, and grace for grace"* (John 1:16).

All the fullness of Christ! Do you know what that is? Do you understand that phrase? I assert that you do not comprehend it, and will not just yet. All the fullness of Christ—the abundance of which you may infer from the depth of your own emptiness—all that fullness is yours to supply your multiplied necessities. All the fullness of Christ is yours—to restrain you, keep you, and preserve you. All that fullness of power and love and purity, which is stored up in the Lord Jesus Christ, is yours. Do treasure that thought, for then your emptiness will never be a cause of fear. How can you be lost while you have all that fullness to go to?

In His Very Life

Now I come to something even sweeter: the very life of Christ is the property of the believer. This is a thought into which I cannot dive, and I feel I have outdone myself in only mentioning it. The life of Christ is the property of every believer. Can you conceive what Christ's life is? "Of course," you say, "He poured it out upon the cross." He did, and it was His life that He then gave to you. However, He took that life up again; even the life of His body was restored.

Yet, the life of His great and glorious divinity had never undergone any change, even at the time of His death. Now, you know He is immortal, for *"only* [He] *hath immortality"* (1 Timothy 6:16). Can you conceive what kind of life it is that the second person of the Trinity possesses? Can He ever die? No, far sooner may the harps of heaven be stopped and the chorus of the redeemed cease forever, far sooner may the glorious walls of paradise be shaken and its foundations be removed, than that God the Son should ever die. As immortal as His Father, Christ now sits at the Father's right hand (Colossians 3:1), the Eternal One.

Christian, that life of Christ is yours. Hear what Jesus said: *"Because I live, ye shall live also"* (John 14:19). *"Ye are dead, and your life is hid with Christ in God"* (Colossians 3:3). The same blow that would strike us dead, spiritually, would have to slay Christ at the same time. The same sword that would take away the spiritual life of a regenerate man would also have to take away the life of the Redeemer. Our lives and His life are intricately linked together—they are not two lives, but one. We are but the rays of the great Sun of Righteousness, our Redeemer—sparks that must return to the great orb again. If we are indeed the true heirs of heaven, we cannot die until He from whom we take our life dies also. We are the stream that cannot stop until the fountain dries up; we are the rays that cannot cease until the sun ceases to shine. We are the branches, and we cannot wither until the trunk itself dies. *"Because I live, ye shall live also."* The very life of Christ is the possession of every one of His own.

In His Person

Best of all, the person of Jesus Christ is the property of the Christian. I am persuaded, beloved, that we think a great deal more of God's gifts than we do of God, and we preach a great deal more about the Holy Spirit's influence than we do about the Holy Spirit. I am also certain that we talk a great deal more about the offices and works and attributes of Christ than we do about the person of Christ.

The reason that few of us can understand the metaphors that are used in Solomon's Song concerning the person of Christ is because we have seldom sought to see Him or desired to know Him. But, believer, you have sometimes been able to behold your Lord. Have you not seen Him, who *"is white and ruddy, the chiefest among ten thousand,...*[and] *altogether lovely"* (Song 5:10, 16)? Have you not been lost in pleasure sometimes when you have seen His head, which is *"as the most fine gold"* (Song 5:11)? Have you not beheld Him in His dual character: the white and the red; the lily and the rose (Song 2:1); the God and yet the man; the dying and yet the living; the perfect One and yet the One who bears *"about in* [His] *body the dying"* (2 Corinthians 4:10)? Have you ever beheld the Lord with the nail prints in His hands and the scar still on His side? And have you ever longed to behold His loving smile or to hear His sweet voice (Song 2:14)? Have you ever had love visits from Him? Has He ever put His banner of love over you (v. 4)? Have you ever gone with Him into the fields and the villages (Song 7:11) and the garden of nuts (Song 6:11)? Have you ever *"sat down under his shadow with great delight"*? Have you ever found that *"his fruit was sweet to* [your] *taste"* (Song 2:3)? Yes, you have. His person, then, is yours.

A wife loves her husband. She loves his house and his property. She loves him for all that he gives her, all the bounty he confers, and all the love he bestows. But, his person is the object of her affections. So it is with the believer: he blesses Christ for all He does and all He is, but it is Christ that is everything to him. The believer does not care as much about Christ's offices as he does about Christ Himself.

Imagine a child on his father's knee. The father is a professor at the university, a learned man with many titles. Perhaps the child knows that these are honorable titles and esteems him for them; but the chid does not care as much about the professor and his dignity as he does about the person of his father. It is not the collegiate square cap or the gown that the child loves. Further, if the child is loving, the meals the father provides or the house in which the child lives will not be as important to the child as is the father whom the child loves. It is the father's dear person that has become the object of true and hearty affection for the child.

Likewise, I am sure it is so with you, if you know your Savior. You love His mercies, you love His offices, you love His deeds, but you love His person best. Take a moment to reflect, then, that the person of Christ is conveyed to you in the covenant: *"I will...give thee for a covenant of the people."*

THE PURPOSES OF CHRIST IN THE COVENANT

Now, let us turn our attention to the second point of consideration: For what purposes did God put Christ in the covenant?

To Provide Comfort for Repentant Sinners

In the first place, Christ is in the covenant in order to comfort every repentant sinner. "Oh," says the sinner who is coming to God, "I cannot lay hold of such a great covenant as that. I cannot believe that heaven is provided for me. I cannot conceive that that robe of righteousness and all these wondrous things can be intended for such a wretch as I am." Comfort comes in the thought that Christ is in the covenant. Sinner, are you able to lay hold of Christ and His cross? You are if you can say,

> Nothing in my hand I bring,
> Simply to Your cross I cling.

If you have laid hold of Christ, then He was put into the covenant on purpose so that you would be able to hold on fast to Him. God's covenant mercies all go together, and if you have laid hold of Christ, you have gained every blessing in the covenant. That is one reason why Christ was put there.

Why, if Christ were not there, the poor sinner would say, "I dare not seize upon that mercy. It is a godly and a divine one, but I dare not fasten my hope on it, because it is too good for me. I cannot receive it; it staggers my faith." However, the man sees Christ with all the great atonement in the covenant. Christ looks so lovingly at Him and opens His arms so wide, saying so kindly, *"Come unto me, all ye that labour and are heavy laden, and I will give you rest"* (Matthew 11:28), that the sinner comes and wraps his arms around Christ in response. Then Christ whispers, "Sinner, in laying hold of Me, you have laid hold of all." The sinner cries, "Lord, I dare not think I could have any other mercies. I dare to trust You, but I dare not take the others." And Christ replies, "Oh, sinner, in that you have taken hold of Me, you have taken all the other mercies, too."

The mercies of the covenant are linked together as in a chain. The one link of Christ is an enticing one. The sinner can lay hold of Him, and God has purposely put Him there to entice the sinner to come and receive the mercies of the covenant. For when the sinner has once grasped hold of Christ—and here is the comfort—he has everything that the covenant can give.

To Reassure the Doubting Saint

Christ was also put in the covenant to confirm the doubting saint. Sometimes the wavering one cannot comprehend his share in the covenant. He cannot imagine that his allotment is with those who are sanctified. He is afraid that God is not his God and that the Spirit has no dealings with his soul. But then,

> Amid temptations, sharp and strong,
>   His soul to that dear refuge flies;
> Hope is his anchor, firm and strong,
>   When tempests blow and billows rise.

And so, that poor, uncertain child lays hold of Christ. Were it not for that, even the believer would not dare to come at all. He could not lay hold of any other mercy than that with which Christ is connected. "Oh," he says, "I know I am a sinner, and Christ came to save sinners." Therefore, he holds fast to Christ. "I can hold fast here," he says; "My black hands will not blacken Christ; my filthiness will not make Him unclean." So the saint holds on tightly to Christ, as tightly as if his grip were the death-clutch of a drowning man. And what then? Why, he has got every mercy of the covenant in his hand.

God, in His wisdom, has put Christ in the covenant of grace. Thus, any poor sinner or any doubting saint, who might be afraid to lay hold of any other, but who knows the gracious nature of Christ, is not afraid to lay hold of Him. Thus, even though he might be totally unaware of it, he grasps the whole of the covenant to himself.

To Give Substance to Many Blessings

Further, it was necessary that Christ should be in the covenant, because there are many things there that would be nothing without Him. Our great redemption is in the covenant, but we have no redemption except through His blood. It is true that my righteousness is in the covenant, but I can have no righteousness apart from that which Christ has won for me, and which is imputed to me by God. It is very true that my eternal perfection is in the covenant, but the elect are only perfect in Christ. They are not perfect in themselves, nor will they ever be, until they have been washed and sanctified and perfected by the Holy Spirit. Even in heaven, the perfection of the saints in glory does not consist so much in their sanctification as it does in their justification in Christ.

> Their beauty this, their glorious dress,
> Jesus the Lord their righteousness.

In fact, if you were to take Christ out of the covenant, you would do the same as if you would break the string of a necklace: all the jewels or beads or pearls would drop off and scatter all over, separating from each other. Christ is the golden string on which the mercies of the covenant are threaded, and when you lay hold of Him, you have obtained the whole string of pearls. However, if Christ were to be taken away, it is true that the pearls would still be there, but we would not be able to wear them or grasp them. They would be separated, and poor faith would never know how to get hold of them. Oh, this is a mercy that is worth worlds: Christ is in the covenant!

To Be Used by the Saints

Notice once more—just as I wrote concerning God in the covenant—Christ is in the covenant to be used. God never gives His children a promise that

He does not intend for them to use. There are some promises in the Bible that I have never yet availed myself of. However, I am sure that there will come times of trial and trouble when I will find that a long-neglected promise, which I thought was never meant for me, will be the only one on which I can rest. I also know that the time is coming when every believer will know the worth of every promise in the covenant. God has not given His children any part of the inheritance that He did not intend for them to make use of. Christ has been given to us to use. Believer, use Him!

I tell you again, as I told you before, that you do not use your Christ as you ought to do. When you are in trouble, why do you not go and tell Him? Has He not a sympathizing heart, and can He not comfort you and alleviate your pain? No, you are gadding about to all your friends except to your Best Friend, and telling your tale everywhere except into the heart of your Lord. Oh, use Him, use Him.

Are you black with yesterday's sins? Here is a fountain filled with blood; use it, saint, use it. Has your guilt returned again? Well, His power has been proved again and again; come, use Him! Use Him! Do you feel naked? Come near, soul, and take *"the robe of righteousness"* (Isaiah 61:10). Do not stand there staring at it; put it on. Strip your own righteousness off, and your own fears, too. Put this on instead. Wear it, for it was meant to be worn.

Do you feel sick? Will you not go and pull the night-bell of prayer to wake up the Great Physician? I urge you to go and appeal to Him, and He will give the medicine that will revive you. What? Are you sick, with the Great Physician next door to you, *"a very present help in* [time of] *trouble"* (Psalm 46:1), and will you not go to Him?

Oh, dearly beloved, remember that you may be poor, but then you have *"a kinsman* [Redeemer], *a mighty man of wealth"* (Ruth 2:1). What! Will you not go to Him and ask Him to give you of His abundance, when He has given you this promise: that as long as He has anything, you will share with Him, for all He is and all He has is yours?

Oh, believer, do use Christ, I urge you. There is nothing Christ dislikes more than for His people to make a showpiece of Him and not to use Him. He loves to be worked. He is a great laborer; He always was for His Father, and now He loves to be a great laborer for His sheep.

The more burdens you put on His shoulders, the better He will love you. *"Cast...all your care upon him; for he careth for you"* (1 Peter 5:7). You will never know the sympathy of Christ's heart and the love of His soul so well as when you have heaved a mountain of trouble from yourself to His shoulders and have found that He does not stagger under the weight. Are your troubles like huge mountains weighing upon your spirit? Command them to rumble like an avalanche upon the shoulders of the Almighty Christ. He can bear all of your troubles away and cast them *"into the depths of the sea"* (Micah 7:19), just as He does with your sins.

Do cry out to your Lord and Master, and use Him. For this very purpose Christ was put into the covenant, that you might use Him whenever you need Him.

A PRINCIPLE OF RECIPROCAL RELATIONSHIP

Finally, here is a principle that can be inferred from what we have learned, and what is that precept? Since Christ is yours, then you are Christ's, beloved. You are Christ's, you know very well. You are His by your Father's gift when He gave you to the Son. You are His by His bloody purchase, when He paid the price for your redemption. You are His by dedication, for you have dedicated yourself to Him. You are His by adoption, for you were brought to Him and made one of His siblings and a joint-heir with Him.

Therefore, dear friend, I urge you to endeavor to show the world that you are His in practice. When tempted to sin, reply, "I cannot do this great wickedness. I cannot, for I am one of Christ's." When wealth is before you to be won by sin, touch it not. Say that you are Christ's; otherwise, you would take it, but now you cannot. Tell Satan that you would not gain the world if you had to love Christ less.

Are you exposed to difficulties and dangers in the world? Stand fast in the evil day (Ephesians 6:13), remembering that you are one of Christ's. Are you working in a job where much is to be done, but others are sitting around idly and lazily, doing nothing? Go to your work, and when the sweat stands upon your brow and you are tempted to stop, say, "No, I cannot; I am one of Christ's. He had a baptism to be baptized with, and so have I, and I am distressed until it is accomplished (Luke 12:50). I am one of Christ's. If I were not one of His and purchased by blood, I might be like Issachar, crouching '*between two burdens*' (Genesis 49:14); but I am one of Christ's." When the siren song of pleasure would tempt you from the path of righteousness, reply, "Hush your strains, O temptress. I am one of Christ's. Your music cannot affect me; I am not my own, for I am bought with a price."

When the cause of God needs you, give yourself to it, for you are Christ's. When the poor need you, give yourself away, for you are one of Christ's. When at any time there is something to be done for His church and for His Cross, do it, remembering that you are one of Christ's. I urge you, never repudiate your profession of faith. Do not go where others could say of you, "He cannot be Christ's." Rather, always be one of those whose dialect is Christian, whose every idiom is Christlike, whose conduct and conversation are so scented with heaven that all who see you will know that you are the Savior's and will recognize in you His features and His lovely countenance.

Now, dearly beloved, I must direct a word to those of you who have not laid hold of the covenant. I sometimes hear it whispered, and sometimes I read it, that there are men who are trusting in the "uncovenanted" mercies of God. Let me solemnly assure you that there is now no such thing in heaven as uncovenanted mercy; there is no such thing beneath God's sky or above it, as uncovenanted grace toward men. All you can receive, and all you ever can hope for, must be through the covenant of free grace, and that alone.

Perhaps, poor convicted sinner, you do not dare to take hold of the covenant today. You cannot say

the covenant is yours. You are afraid it never can be
yours, because you are such an unworthy wretch.
Listen, can you lay hold of Christ? Do you dare to do
that? "Oh," you say, "I am too unworthy." No, that
is not true. Soul, do you dare to touch the hem of His
garment today? Do you dare to come near enough to
Him just to be able to touch the very bottom of His
robe that is trailing on the ground? "No," you say, "I
dare not." Why not, poor soul, why not? Can you not
trust Christ?

> Are not His mercies rich and free?
> Then say, poor soul, why not for thee?

"I dare not come; I am so unworthy," you say.
Hear to this, for my Master invites you to come:
*"Come unto me, all ye that labour and are heavy
laden, and I will give you rest"* (Matthew 11:28). Are
you still afraid after that? *"This is a faithful saying,
and worthy of all acceptation, that Christ Jesus came
into the world to save sinners"* (1 Timothy 1:15).

Why, then, do you not come to Christ? Oh, are
you afraid He will turn you away? Listen, then, to
what He said: "[Whoever] *cometh to me I will in no
wise cast out"* (John 6:37). You say, "But I know He
would cast me out." Come, then, and see if you can
prove Him a liar. I know you cannot, but come and
try. Christ has said that He will not reject anyone
who comes to Him. "But I am the blackest." Nevertheless, He has said *"him that cometh"* (v. 37), and
that includes you, as long as you come to Him, no
matter what condition you are in. Come along,
blackest of the black. "Oh, but I am so filthy!" Come
along, filthy one, come and try Him. Come and prove

Him; remember that He has said He will cast out none that come to Him by faith.

Come and try Him. I am not asking you to lay hold of the whole covenant right now—you will do that soon enough—but just to lay hold of Christ. If you will do that, then you will have the covenant. "Oh, I cannot lay hold of Him," says one poor soul. Well then, lie prostrate at His feet and beg Him to lay hold of you. Groan one groan, and say, *"God be merciful to me a sinner"* (Luke 18:13). Sigh one sigh, and say, "Lord, save me, or I will perish" (Matthew 8:25). Let your heart say it, even if your lips cannot. If grief, long smothered, burns like a flame within your bones, at least let one spark out.

Now pray one prayer, and—I am telling you the truth—that one sincere prayer will most assuredly prove that He will save you. One true groan, when God has put it in your heart, is a deposit of His love. One true wish for Christ, if it is followed by a sincere and earnest seeking of Him, will be accepted by God, and you will be saved.

Come, soul, lay hold of Christ. "Oh, but I dare not!" Now, I was about to express a foolish thing: I was going to write that I wish I were a sinner like you now, because I would run before you, lay hold of Christ, and then say to you, "Take hold of Him, too." However, I am a sinner like yourself, and no better than yourself. I have no merits, no righteousness, no works. I will be damned in hell unless Christ has mercy on me, and I should have been there now if I had been given what was rightfully due me.

Here am I, a sinner once as black as you are. Yet, I can say, "O Christ, these arms embrace You."

Sinner, come and take your turn after me. Have I not embraced Him? Am I not as vile as you are? Come, and let my case assure you. How did He treat me when I first laid hold of Him? Why, He said to me, *"I have loved thee with an everlasting love: therefore with lovingkindness have I drawn thee"* (Jeremiah 31:3). Come, sinner, come and try. If Christ did not drive me away, He will never spurn you. Come along, poor soul, come along.

> Venture on Him ('tis no venture),
> Venture wholly,
> Let no other trust intrude;
> None but Jesus
> Can do helpless sinners good.

He can do for you all the good you need. Oh, trust my Master, trust my Master. He is a precious Lord Jesus, He is a sweet Lord Jesus, He is a loving Savior, and He is a kind and condescending forgiver of sin. Come, you black; come, you filthy; come, you poor; come, you dying; come, you lost—you who have been taught to feel your need of Christ—come, all of you. Come now because Jesus invites you to come! Come quickly! Lord Jesus, draw them, draw them by Your Spirit!

Chapter 4

The Holy Spirit in the Covenant

And I will put my spirit within you.
—Ezekiel 36:27

The Holy Spirit is the third person of the Trinity and in the covenant. We have already considered "God in the Covenant" and "Christ in the Covenant." At this time, we will consider God the Holy Spirit's involvement in the covenant. Remember, it was necessary that the Triune God should work out the salvation of the elect, if they were to be saved at all. It was also absolutely requisite that, when the covenant was made, all that was necessary should be put into it. This included, among the rest, the Holy Spirit, without whom all things done even by the Father and by Jesus Christ would have been ineffectual. The Spirit is as much a

79

part of the covenant as the Savior of men or the Father of spirits.

Today, when the Holy Spirit is too much forgotten, and when only a little honor is accorded to His sacred person, I know that there is a deep responsibility upon me to endeavor to magnify His great and holy name. I almost tremble, right now, in entering on so profound a subject, for which I feel myself so insufficient. But, nevertheless, relying on the aid, the guidance, and the witness of the Holy Spirit Himself, I will venture to explain our text: *"I will put my spirit within you."*

In the covenant of grace, the Holy Spirit is given to all the children of God and is received by each, in due course. Yet, upon our Lord Jesus Christ did the Holy Spirit first descend, resting upon Christ (Matthew 3:16) as our covenant Head, *"like the precious ointment upon the head, that ran down upon the beard, even Aaron's beard: that went down to the skirts of his garments"* (Psalm 133:2). The Father gave the Holy Spirit without measure to His Son (John 3:34).

From Jesus, in a measured amount, although still in abundance, all the *"brethren* [who] *dwell together in unity"* (Psalm 133:1), or union with Him, partake of the Holy Spirit. This holy anointing of the Spirit flows down from Christ, the Anointed One, to every part of His body, to every individual member of His church. The Father's declaration concerning Christ was this: *"Behold my servant, whom I have chosen; my beloved, in whom* [I am] *well pleased: I will put my spirit upon him"* (Matthew 12:18). And Christ said,

> [18] *The Spirit of the Lord is upon me, because he hath anointed me to preach the gospel to the poor; he hath sent me to heal the brokenhearted, to preach deliverance to the captives, and recovering of sight to the blind, to set at liberty them that are bruised,* [19] *To preach the acceptable year of the Lord.*
>
> (Luke 4:18–19)

Thus, the Holy Spirit was first poured out upon our covenant Head, Jesus Christ. From Him, then, the Spirit descends to all those who are in union with Christ. Let us bless the name of Jesus if we are united with Him, and let us look up to our covenant Head, expecting that from Him will flow down the heavenly ointment that will consecrate our souls— the anointing of the Spirit.

Our text is one of the unconditional promises of Scripture. There are many conditional promises in the Word of God given to certain biblical characters, although even those promises are in some sense unconditional, since the very condition of the promise is by some other promise secured as a gift. However, this one has no conditions whatever. It does not say, "I will put My Spirit within you if you ask for Him or if you seek Him with all your heart." Rather, it says plainly, without any reservations or stipulations, *"I will put my spirit within you."* The reason is obvious. Until the Spirit is put within us, we cannot feel our need of the Spirit, and neither can we ask for or seek Him.

Therefore, it is necessary that there should be an absolutely unconditional promise, made to all the chosen of God, that they should have given to them the waiting grace, the desiring grace, the seeking grace, the receiving grace, the believing grace, that will make them pant and hunger and thirst after Jesus. To everyone who is *"chosen of God, and precious"* (1 Peter 2:4), to every redeemed soul, however much he is now condemningly sunk in sin, however much he is now lost and ruined by the Fall, however much he may hate God and despise his Redeemer at the present moment, this promise still holds true: *"I will put my spirit within you."* In due course, all of the redeemed will be instilled with the Holy Spirit, who will quicken their spirits from spiritual death, lead them to seek pardon, induce them to trust in Jesus Christ, and adopt them into the living family of God.

The promise also concerns an internal blessing that will be bestowed: *"I will put my spirit within you."* Remember, we have the Spirit of God in His written Word. We also find the Spirit in the ordinances of baptism and the Lord's Supper, which are administered by every faithful minister of the Gospel. God is perpetually giving the Spirit to us by these means. However, it is in vain for us to hear of the Spirit, to talk of Him, or to believe in Him, unless we have a realization of His power within us. Here, therefore, is the promise of such an internal blessing: *"I will put my spirit within you."*

We will now consider this promise in all of its comprehensiveness. May the Holy Spirit Himself assist us in doing this! We will take the various works of the Holy Spirit, one by one, and we will remember that, in all the works that He performs, the Holy Spirit is put in the covenant to be possessed by every believer.

THE HOLY SPIRIT AS OUR QUICKENER

In the first place, Christ told us, *"It is the spirit that quickeneth"* (John 6:63). Until the Holy Spirit is pleased to breathe upon a soul, that person is dead to any spiritual life. It is not until the Holy Spirit, like some heavenly wind, breathes upon the dry bones and puts life into them (Ezekiel 37:6) that they can ever live. You may take a corpse and dress it in all the garments of external decency. You may wash it with the water of morality. You may adorn the corpse with the crown of glory and put upon its brow a tiara of beauty. You may paint its cheeks until you make it appear lifelike. But, remember, unless its spirit is alive, corruption will seize the body before too long.

Therefore, beloved, it is the Holy Spirit who is the Quickener. You would have been as *"dead in trespasses and sins"* (Ephesians 2:1) now as you ever were, if it had not been for the Holy Spirit who made you alive. You were not simply lying, *"cast out in the open field"* (Ezekiel 16:5), but, worse than that, you were the very prey of mortality. Corruption was your father; the worm was your mother and your sister (Job 17:14). You were noxious in the nostrils of the Almighty.

It was as the Savior beheld you in that deplorable state, in all your loathsomeness, that He said to you, *"Live"* (Ezekiel 16:6). In that moment, you were *"begotten...again unto a lively hope by the resurrection of Jesus Christ from the dead"* (1 Peter 1:3). Life entered into you at His command. Then it was that the Holy Spirit quickened your spirit. As Jesus told

His disciples, *"The words that I speak unto you, they are spirit, and they are life"* (John 6:63). You were made alive entirely through the might and power of the quickening Spirit.

> The Spirit, like some heavenly wind,
> Blows on the sons of flesh;
> Creates a new—a heavenly mind,
> And forms the man afresh.

If, then, you feel at any time death working in you, as doubtless you will, withering the bloom of your piety, chilling the fervor of your devotions, and quenching the ardor of your faith, remember that He who first quickened you must keep you alive. The Holy Spirit's quickening power is the sap that flowed flowed into your poor, dry branch, when you were grafted into Christ. (See Romans 11:16–17.) Just as, by that sap, you were first made green with life, so it is by that sap alone you can ever bring forth fruit unto God. By the Spirit you drew your first breath when you cried out for mercy, and from the same Spirit you must draw the breath to praise that mercy in hymns and anthems of joy.

"Having begun in the Spirit" (Galatians 3:3), you must be made perfect in the Spirit, for perfection cannot come from the flesh. *"The flesh profiteth nothing"* (John 6:63); the works of the law will not help you; your own heart's thoughts and devices are of no avail. You would be cut off from Christ; you would be more depraved than you were before your conversion; you would be more corrupt than you were prior to your being regenerated—*"twice dead, plucked up by the roots"* (Jude 1:12)—if God the

Holy Spirit were to withdraw from you. You must live in His life, trust in His power to sustain you, and seek of Him fresh supplies when the tide of your spiritual life is running low.

THE HOLY SPIRIT AS OUR HELPER

We need the Holy Spirit as our able Helper in all the duties we have to perform. We all need *"to be strengthened with might by his Spirit"* (Ephesians 3:16) to do the *"good works, which God hath before ordained that we should walk in them"* (Ephesians 2:10). *"I will pray the Father, and he shall give you another* [Paraclete or Helper], *that he may abide with you for ever; even the Spirit of truth;...he dwelleth with you, and shall be in you"* (John 14:16–17). *"Likewise the Spirit also helpeth our infirmities"* (Romans 8:26).

An Aide in Prayer

The most common Christian duty is that of prayer, and the most insignificant child of God must be a praying child. Remember that the passage in Romans continues this way:

> [26] *Likewise the Spirit also helpeth our infirmities: for we know not what we should pray for as we ought: but the Spirit itself maketh intercession for us with groanings which cannot be uttered.*
> [27] *And he that searcheth the hearts knoweth what is the mind of the Spirit, because he maketh intercession for the saints according to the will of God.* (Romans 8:26–27)

The Spirit of God is in the covenant as the great Aide to us in all our petitions to the throne of grace. Child of God, you do not know what to pray for; depend on the inspiration of the Holy Spirit, who will teach you how to pray. Sometimes you do not know how to express what you desire; rely upon the Spirit, then, as the One who can touch your lips with the *"live coal...from off the altar"* (Isaiah 6:6), because then you will be able to pour out your fervent wishes before the throne. Sometimes, even when you have life and power within you, you cannot express your inward emotions; then rely upon that Spirit to interpret your feelings, for He *"maketh intercession for us with groanings which cannot be uttered."* When, like Jacob, you are wrestling with the angel and are nearly thrown down, ask the Holy Spirit to strengthen your arms.

The Holy Spirit is the chariot wheel of prayer. Prayer may be the chariot, and desire may pull it forward, but the Spirit is the wheel by which it moves. He propels the desire and causes the chariot to roll swiftly on, carrying to heaven the supplication of the saints, when the desire of the heart is *"according to the will of God."*

An Aide in Preaching

Another duty to which some of the children of God are called is that of preaching. Here also we must have the Holy Spirit to enable us. Those whom God calls to preach the Gospel are assisted with might from on high. He has said, *"Lo, I am with you alway, even unto the end of the world"* (Matthew

28:20). It is a solemn thing to enter into the work of the ministry.

I will just make an observation here, for there are young men who are striving to enter into the ministry before they scarcely know the alphabet of the Gospel. They set themselves up as preachers of God's Word, when the first thing they ought to do is to join the kindergarten class in a school and learn to read properly.

I know there are some to whom God has given the desire thus to seek the glory of His name and the welfare of souls, and they humbly wait until He has opened the way. May God bless them and speed them in answering His call. But—would you believe it?—I know a young man who was baptized and received into the church one Sunday, and who went off to a seminary the next day to ask if they would accept him! I asked him whether he had ever preached before or addressed half-a-dozen Sunday school students. He said that he had not. But what surprised me most was that he said he was called to the work before he was converted! I truly believe this was a call from the Enemy—not a call from God in the slightest sense.

Be careful that you do not touch God's ark of the covenant with unholy fingers. You may preach if you can, but take care that you do not set yourself up in the ministry without having a solemn conviction that the Spirit from on high has set you apart for that vocation. If you do, *"in thy skirts* [will be] *found the blood of the souls of the poor innocents"* (Jeremiah 2:34). Too many have rushed into the Holy Place without being called by God; and if they could have rushed out of it on their deathbeds, they would have had eternal cause for gratitude. However, they ran presumptuously, then preached unsent, and therefore unblessed. When dying, they felt a greater condemnation from the fact that they had taken on themselves an office to which God had never appointed them. Beware of doing that.

But, if God has called you, however little talent you may have, do not fear anyone's frown or rebuke. If you have a solemn conviction in your soul that God has really ordained you to the work of the ministry, and if you have obtained a seal to your commission in the conversion of even one soul, do not let death or hell stop you. Go straight on, and never think you must have certain endowments to become a successful preacher.

The only endowment necessary for success in the ministry is the endowment of the Holy Spirit. As I was addressing a number of ministers recently, I told the brothers there, when one of them asked how it was that God had been pleased to bless me so much in my ministry, "There is not one of you whom God could not bless ten times as much, if you had ten times as much of the Spirit." It is not any ability of the preacher nor any human qualification that brings the blessing; it is simply the influence of God's Spirit that is necessary.

I have been delighted to find myself labeled as ignorant, unlearned, and devoid of eloquence, all of which I knew long before those titles were given to me. But so much the better, for then all the glory belongs to God. Let men say what they please, I will always confess to the truth of it: I am a fool. *"I am become a fool in glorying"* (2 Corinthians 12:11), if you please. I will take any contemptible title that worldlings like to put upon me. However, they cannot deny the fact that God blesses my ministry, that prostitutes have been saved, that drunkards have been reclaimed, that some of the most forsaken characters have been changed, and that God has produced such a work in their midst as my critics have never seen before in their lives. Therefore, give all the glory to His holy name. Cast as much reproach as you like on me, you worldlings; it only brings more honor to God, who works as He pleases and with whatever instrument He chooses, irrespective of man's opinions.

An Aide in Every Endeavor

Again, dearly beloved, whatever your vocation is, whatever God has ordained you to do in this world, you are equally certain to have the assistance of the Holy Spirit in it. If it is the teaching of a nursery class in the Sunday school, do not think that the Holy Spirit will not help you. His support will be granted as freely to you as to the person who addresses a large assembly. Are you sitting down by the side of some poor, dying woman? Believe that the Holy Spirit will come to you there, as much as if you were administering the sacred elements of the Lord's Supper. Seek strength from God as much for the humblest work as for the loftiest. Spiritual plowman, sharpen your plowshare with the Spirit! Spiritual sower, dip your seed in the Spirit, so it will germinate, and ask the Spirit to give you grace to scatter it so that it may fall *"into good ground"* (Matthew 13:8)! Spiritual warrior, sharpen your sword with the Spirit, and ask Him, whose Word is a two-edged sword (Hebrews 4:12), to strengthen your arm to wield it!

THE HOLY SPIRIT AS OUR REVEALER

The next point we will discuss is that the Holy Spirit is given to the children of God as *"the spirit of wisdom and revelation in the knowledge of* [God]*"* (Ephesians 1:17). The Spirit brings us *"out of darkness into his marvellous light"* (1 Peter 2:9). By nature, we are ignorant, extremely so, but the Holy Spirit teaches the family of God and makes them wise. *"Ye have an unction from the Holy One, and ye know all things"* (1 John 2:20).

Student in the school of Christ, do you want to be wise? Then, do not ask the theologian to expound to you his system of divinity. Instead, sitting down meekly at the feet of Jesus, ask that His Spirit may instruct you. For I tell you, student, that although you might read the Bible for many years and turn over its pages continually, you will not learn anything of its hidden mysteries without the revelation of the Holy Spirit. Yet, in a solitary moment of your study, when suddenly enlightened by the Spirit, you may learn a truth as swiftly as you see the lightning flash.

Young person, are you striving to understand the doctrine of election? It is the Holy Spirit alone who can reveal it to your heart and make you comprehend it. Are you struggling to grasp the doctrine of human depravity? The Holy Spirit must reveal to you the depth of the wickedness of the human heart. Do you really desire to know the secret of the life of the believer, as he lives *"by the faith of the Son of God"* (Galatians 2:20), and the mysterious fellowship with the Lord that he enjoys? It will always be a mystery to you unless the Holy Spirit unfolds it to your heart.

Whenever you read the Bible, cry to the Spirit, *"Open thou mine eyes, that I may behold wondrous things out of thy law"* (Psalm 119:18). The Spirit gives heavenly eye salve to those who are spiritually blind. If your eyes are not open now, seek the eye salve, and you will see—yes, and see so clearly that he who has only been educated in man's school will ask, *"How knoweth this man letters, having never learned?"* (John 7:15).

Those who are taught by the Holy Spirit often surpass those who are taught by man. I once met an entirely uneducated country bumpkin who never went to school for one hour in his life, yet who knew more about the Holy Scriptures than many clergymen who have received advanced training at the finest seminaries. I have been told that it is a common practice for men in Wales, while they are at work breaking stones in the quarries, to discuss difficult points in theology, which many a theologian cannot master. Their understanding is enlightened because they humbly read the Scriptures, trusting only in the guidance of the Holy Spirit and believing that *"when he, the Spirit of truth, is come, he will guide* [them] *into all truth"* (John 16:13). And the Holy Spirit is pleased to do so.

91

All other instruction is very good. Solomon said, *"That the soul be without knowledge, it is not good"* (Proverbs 19:2). We should all seek to know as much as can be known. Yet, let us remember that in the work of salvation, real knowledge must be obtained by the teaching of the Holy Spirit. If we would learn in the heart, and not merely in the head, we must be taught entirely by the Holy Spirit. What you learn from man, you can unlearn; but what you learn from the Spirit is fixed indelibly in your heart and your conscience, and not even Satan himself can steal it from you. Go, you ignorant ones, who often shy away from the truths of revelation. Go, and ask the Spirit, for He is the Guide of unenlightened souls and the Guide of His own enlightened people. Without His aid, even when they have been *"once enlightened, and have tasted of the heavenly gift"* (Hebrews 6:4), they could not understand all truth unless the Spirit led them into it.

THE HOLY SPIRIT AS OUR APPLIER

God also gives the Holy Spirit to us as the Spirit of Application. Thus it was that Jesus said to His disciples, *"He shall glorify me: for he shall receive of mine, and shall show it unto you"* (John 16:14). To make the matter clearer still, our Lord added, *"All things that the Father hath are mine: therefore said I, that he shall take of mine, and shall show it unto you"* (v. 15). Let me remind you how frequently Jesus impressed on His disciples the fact that He spoke to them the words of His Father: *"Jesus answered them, and said, My doctrine is not mine, but his that sent me"* (John 7:16). Again, He said, *"The words that I speak unto you I speak not of myself: but the Father that dwelleth in me, he doeth the works"* (John 14:10).

As Christ thus made known the will of God the Father to His people, so the Holy Spirit makes known to us the words of Christ. I could almost affirm that Christ's words would be of no use to us if they were not instilled in us by the Holy Spirit. Beloved, we need this application to assure our hearts that His words belong to us, that they are intended for us, and that we have a share in their blessedness. Further, we need the anointing of the Spirit to make them bedew our hearts and refresh our souls.

Did you ever have a promise applied to your heart? Do you understand what is meant by *application* as the exclusive work of the Spirit? Just as Paul said the Gospel came to the Thessalonians, it comes to you *"not...in word only, but also in power, and in the Holy Ghost, and in much assurance"* (1 Thessalonians 1:5).

Sometimes the Spirit's application comes suddenly. Your heart may have been the scene of a thousand distracting thoughts, wave after wave crashing upon your mind, until the tempest rose beyond your control. And then, some text of Scripture, like a mighty decree from the lips of Jesus, has stilled your troubled soul. Immediately, there has been a great calm, and you have wondered where it came from. The sweet passage has rung like music in your ears; like a wafer made of honey, the Scripture has moistened your tongue; like a charm, it has quelled your anxieties. It has stayed uppermost in your thoughts all day long, reining in all your lawless passions and restless strivings. Perhaps it has continued in your mind for weeks; wherever you went, whatever you did, you could not dislodge it, nor did you wish to do so, because it was so sweet and so savory to your soul. Have you not thought of such a text that it is the best in the Bible, the most precious in all the Holy Scriptures? That was because it was so graciously applied to you by the Holy Spirit.

Oh, how I love applied promises! I might read a thousand promises as they stand recorded on the pages of the Sacred Volume, and yet get nothing from them. My heart would not burn within me, even for all their richness. Yet, one promise, brought home to my soul by the Spirit's application, has such *"marrow and fatness"* (Psalm 63:5) in it that it would be food enough for forty days for many of the Lord's Elijahs. How sweet it is, in times of deep affliction and trial, to have this promise applied to one's heart:

> ² *When thou passest through the waters, I will be with thee; and through the rivers, they shall not overflow thee: when thou walkest through the fire, thou shalt not be burned; neither shall the flame kindle upon thee.*   (Isaiah 43:2)

Perhaps you are saying, "Oh, that is all just emotionalism." Of course, it appears that way to you, if you, in the natural, cannot discern the things of the Spirit. But we are talking about spiritual things to spiritually-minded men (1 Corinthians 2:13–14). To them this is not merely emotionalism;

it is often a matter of life or death. I have known numerous cases where the only plank on which a poor, troubled believer was able to float was just one verse, on which he had, somehow or other, so tightened his grasp that nothing could take it away from him.

Nor is it only the Word of our Lord that needs to be applied to our hearts. *"The Spirit of truth...shall receive of mine, and shall show it unto you"* (John 16:13–14) may likewise refer to our Savior's precious blood. We sometimes sing,

> There is a fountain filled with blood
> Drawn from Immanuel's veins.

We talk of bathing in that blood-filled reservoir. Now, faith does not apply the blood of Christ to the soul; that is the work of the Spirit. Yes, it is true that I seek it by faith, but it is the Spirit who washes me in the *"fountain opened...for sin and for uncleanness"* (Zechariah 13:1).

It is the Holy Spirit who receives the things of Christ and shows them to us. We would never have a drop of blood sprinkled on our hearts if it were not sprinkled there by the Holy Spirit. So, too, the robe of Christ's righteousness is fitted on us entirely by the Spirit. We are not invited to appropriate the obedience of Christ for ourselves, but the Spirit brings everything to us that Christ has made available for us. Ask the Spirit, then, that you may have the Word applied, the blood applied, pardon applied, and grace applied. You will not be asking in vain, because God Almighty has promised, *"I will put my spirit within you."*

THE HOLY SPIRIT AS OUR SANCTIFIER

Now, we need to note another very important point: we must receive the Spirit as our Sanctifier. Perhaps this is one of the greatest works of the Holy Spirit—sanctifying the soul. It is a great work to purge the soul from sin: it is greater than if one could wash a leopard until all his spots were obliterated, or an Ethiopian until his sable skin became white (Jeremiah 13:23). Our sins are more than skin-deep—they have entered into our very nature. If our exteriors were washed pure and clean right now, we would be polluted before tomorrow; and if all the spots were taken away today, they would grow again tomorrow, for we are sin-stained all the way through. You may scrub the flesh, but we are filthy to the core; our sinfulness is a leprosy that lies deep within.

However, it is the Holy Spirit who sanctifies the soul. He enters the heart, beginning the work of sanctification with conversion. He retains possession of the heart and preserves sanctification by perpetually pouring in the fresh oil of grace, until at last He will perfect sanctification by making the soul pure and spotless, fit to dwell with the blessed inhabitants of glory.

The way the Holy Spirit sanctifies a person is this: first, He reveals to the soul the evil of sin and makes that soul hate it; the Spirit shows sin to be a deadly evil, full of poison. Then, when the soul begins to hate the evil of sin, the next thing the Holy Spirit does is to show that the blood of Christ takes all the guilt away, and, from that very fact, to lead the soul to hate sin even more than he did when he first knew his blackness. The Holy Spirit takes that soul to *"the blood of sprinkling, that speaketh better things than that of Abel"* (Hebrews 12:24). There He tolls the death knell of sin as He points to the blood of Christ and says, "Jesus shed this for you, in order that He might purchase you for Himself, to be one of His *'peculiar people, zealous of good works'"* (Titus 2:14).

Afterward, the Holy Spirit may, at times, allow sin to break out in the heart of the redeemed child of God so that he may be more strongly restrained by greater watchfulness and carefulness in the future. When an heir of heaven does indulge in sin, the Holy Spirit sends a sanctifying chastisement upon his soul until, his heart being broken with deep grief by the pain of the wound, evil is cleansed away. The soul's conscience, feeling uneasy, propels his heart to Christ, who removes the chastisement and takes away the guilt.

Remember, believer, all your holiness is the work of the Holy Spirit. You do not have one grace that the Spirit did not give you, not a solitary virtue that He did not work in you, no goodness that was not given to you by the Spirit. Therefore, never boast of your virtues or of your graces. Are you even-tempered now, where once you were easily angered? Do not brag about it; you will be angry again if the Spirit leaves you. Are you now pure, whereas you were once unclean? Do not flaunt your purity, the seed of which was brought to you from heaven. It never grew within your heart by nature; it is God's gift alone.

Is unbelief prevailing against you? Do your lusts, your evil passions, and your corrupt desires seem likely to master you? Then, I will not say, "Up and at 'em!" but I urge you to cry out mightily to God that you would be filled with the Holy Spirit. Then you will conquer at last and become more than a conqueror (Romans 8:37) over all your sins, because the Lord has promised, *"I will put my spirit within you."*

THE HOLY SPIRIT AS OUR GUIDE

The Spirit of God is promised to the heirs of salvation as a directing Spirit, to guide them in the path of providence. *"When he, the Spirit of truth, is come, he will guide you into all truth"* (John 16:13). *"In all thy ways acknowledge him, and he shall direct thy paths"* (Proverbs 3:6).

If you are ever in a position in which you do not know what road to take, remember that true strength is found in your being at rest, and true wisdom is discovered when you wait for the directing voice of the Spirit, as He says to you, *"This is the way, walk ye in it"* (Isaiah 30:21). I trust that I have learned this principle myself, and I am sure every child of God who has been placed in difficulties must have felt, at times, the reality and blessedness of the Holy Spirit's guidance.

Have you ever prayed that He would direct you? If you have, did you ever find that you went wrong afterward? I do not mean the sort of prayers that are presented by those who ask for counsel, but not of the Lord:

¹ *Woe to the rebellious children, saith the LORD, that take counsel, but not of me; and that cover with a covering, but not of my spirit, that they may add sin to sin:*
² *That walk to go down into Egypt, and have not asked at my mouth; to strengthen themselves in the strength of Pharaoh, and to trust in the shadow of Egypt!*   (Isaiah 30:1–2)

Those rebellious souls ask God to bless them in ways that He never sanctioned. Instead, you must start by renouncing every other trust. Only then can you find proof of His promise: *"Commit thy way unto the LORD; trust also in him; and he shall bring it to pass"* (Psalm 37:5). Child of God, take an open confession with you as you *"come boldly unto the throne of grace"* (Hebrews 4:16). Say, "Lord, I desire, like the wind, to be moved by the breath of the Spirit. Here I am, Lord, passive in Your hand. Happily would I know only Your will. Joyfully I would act according to Your will alone. Show me *'what is* [Your] *good, and acceptable, and perfect, will'* (Romans 12:2), Lord! Teach me what to do and what to refrain from doing."

To some of you, this may seem to be complete fanaticism; you do not believe that God the Holy Spirit ever guides men in the way they should take. And this is the perspective you would be expected to have if you have never experienced His guidance. I have heard that, when an English traveler in Africa told the inhabitants about the intense cold that sometimes prevailed in his country, by which water became so hard that people could skate and walk upon it, the king threatened to put him to death if he told any more lies, for he had never felt or seen such things. What one has never seen or felt is certainly an appropriate subject for doubt and contradiction.

However, regarding those of the Lord's people who tell you that they are led by the Spirit, I advise you to give careful consideration to their words and seek to be so led yourself. It would be a good thing if you were just to go to God as a child in all your distresses. Remember that, as an Advisor whom you may safely consult, as a Guide whose directions you may safely follow, as a Friend on whose protection you may safely rely, the Holy Spirit is personally present in the church of Christ and with each of the disciples of Jesus. And there is no fee to pay except your heartfelt gratitude and praise for His wise direction to you.

THE HOLY SPIRIT AS OUR COMFORTER

The Holy Spirit is given to God's children as a comforting Spirit. This is distinctively His office. Have you never felt that, immediately before a great and grievous trouble, you have had a most unaccountable season of joy? You scarcely knew why you were so happy or so tranquil; you seemed to be floating upon the Sea of Paradise. There was not a breath of wind to ruffle your peaceful spirit; all was serene and calm. You were not agitated by the ordinary cares and anxieties of the world; your whole mind was absorbed in sacred meditation. Later on, when the trouble came, you could say, "Now I understand it all; I could not before comprehend the meaning of that pleasant lull, that quiet happiness; but I see now that it was designed to prepare me for these trying circumstances. If I had been low and dispirited when this trouble burst upon me, it would have broken my heart. But now, thanks be to God, I can perceive through Jesus Christ how this *'light affliction, which is but for a moment,* [is working for me] *a far more exceeding and eternal weight of glory'"* (2 Corinthians 4:17).

I do believe that it is worthwhile to have the troubles in order to get the comfort of the Holy Spirit; it is worthwhile to endure the storm in order to realize the joys.

Sometimes, my heart could have been shaken by derision, shame, and contempt: a fellow minister, of whom I had thought better things, reviled me; a Christian in my congregation turned on his heel and walked away from me because I had been misrepresented to him, and he hated me without cause. However, it has so happened that, at the very time of these incidents, if the whole church had turned its back on me and the whole world had hissed at me, it would not have greatly moved me. Some bright ray of spiritual sunshine filled my heart, and Jesus whispered to me those sweet words, *"I am my beloved's, and my beloved is mine"* (Song 6:3). At such times, the consolations of the Spirit have been neither few nor small with me.

O Christian, if I were able, I would bring you yet further into the depths of this glorious passage; but, as I cannot, I must leave it with you. It is full of honey; only put it to your lips, and get the honey from it. *"I will put my spirit within you."*

THE HOLY SPIRIT AS OUR GRACE

Finally, do you not see here the absolute certainty of the salvation of every believer? Or rather, is it not absolutely certain that every member of the family of God's Israel must be saved? For it is written, *"I will put my spirit within you."* Do you think that when God puts His Spirit within men, they could possibly be damned? Can you dare to think God puts His Spirit into them, and yet they could perish and be lost? You may think so if you please, but I will tell you what God thinks: *"I will put my spirit within you, and cause you to walk in my statutes, and ye shall keep my judgments, and do them"* (Ezekiel 36:27). Sinners are far from God because of their wicked works, and they will not come unto Him that they may have life (John 5:40). Yet, when God says, *"I will put my spirit within you,"* He compels them to come to Him.

What a vain pretense it is to profess to honor God by a doctrine that makes salvation depend on the will of man! If it were true, you might say to God, "We thank you, O Lord, for what You have done; You have given us a great many things, and we offer You Your reward of praise, which is justly due to Your name; but we think we deserve more, for the deciding point was in our free will." Beloved, do not swerve from the free grace of God, for the babblings about man's free agency are neither more nor less than lies, absolutely contrary to the truth of Christ and the teachings of the Spirit.

How certain, then, is the salvation of every elect soul! It does not depend on the will of man; he is made *"willing in the day of* [God's] *power"* (Psalm 110:3). He will be called at the appointed time, and his heart will be completely changed, in order that he may become a trophy of the Redeemer's power. The fact that he was unwilling before then is no hindrance; God gives him the will, so that he is then of a willing mind. Thus, every heir of heaven must be saved, because the Spirit is put within him, and thereby his disposition and affections are molded according to the will of God.

How useless is it for any person to suppose that he can be saved without the Holy Spirit! Dear friend, men sometimes go very near to salvation without being saved, like the poor man who lay beside the pool of Bethesda for thirty-eight years, always close to the water, but never getting in (John 5:2–7). How many changes in outward character there are that very much resemble conversion, yet, these people, not having the Spirit within them, fail after all! Deathbed repentances are often looked upon as very sincere, although too frequently, I fear, they are but the first gnawings of *"their worm* [that] *shall not die"* (Isaiah 66:24).

I have recently read an extraordinary anecdote of a woman who, many years ago, was condemned to death for murdering her child and was hanged in the Grass Market at Edinburgh. She very diligently reformed during the six weeks that were allowed her by Scottish law, previous to her execution. The ministers who were with her continually stated as their opinion that she would die in the sure and certain hope of salvation. The appointed day came, and she was hanged. But, because it was very rainy that day and no awning had been prepared, those who were in charge of her execution were in a great hurry to complete it and get themselves under shelter, so her body was cut down before the legally set time had elapsed. As the custom was, the body was given up to her friends to be buried. A coffin was provided, and she was transported in it to East Lothian, where her husband was going to bury her. Her friends stopped at an inn on the road to refresh themselves, when, to their great surprise and alarm, in rushed a boy who said he heard a noise in the coffin. They went out and found that the woman was alive. Her vital powers had been suspended, but her life was not extinct, and the jolting of the cart had stimulated her to arousal. After a few hours, she was quite revived. She and her husband moved their residence and went to another part of the country.

The sad part of this tale is that the woman was as bad a character after she recovered as she ever had been before, and, if anything, she was worse. She lived just as openly in sin, despising and hating religion even more than she had previously done. Hers was a most remarkable case. Nevertheless, I believe that you can see from it that the great majority of those who profess to repent on their deathbeds, if they could rise again from their graves, would live a life as profane and godless as ever.

Rely on this: it is nothing but the grace of the Spirit of God that makes sure work of your souls. Unless He transforms you, you may be changed, but it will not be a change that will endure. Unless He puts His hand to the work, the work will be marred, the pitcher spoiled on the potter's wheel.

Therefore, cry unto the Lord that He may give you the Holy Spirit, and that you may have the evidence of a real conversion and not a cheap counterfeit. Take heed, sinner, take heed! Natural fear, natural love, natural feelings are not conversion. In the first place, and by all subsequent edification, conversion must be the work of the Holy Spirit, and of Him alone. Never rest comfortably, then, until the Holy Spirit's operations are most surely working in your heart!

Chapter 5

The Blood of the Covenant

*Now the God of peace, that brought again from the
dead our Lord Jesus, that great shepherd of the
sheep, through the blood of the everlasting covenant,
make you perfect in every good work to do his will,
working in you that which is wellpleasing in his
sight, through Jesus Christ; to whom
be glory for ever and ever. Amen.*
—Hebrews 13:20–21

What we ask others to do we should be prepared to do ourselves. Instruction fails unless it is followed by clear example. The
writer had just exhorted the Hebrew believers to
"pray for us" (Hebrews 13:18). Then, as if to show
that he did not ask of them what he was not himself
willing to give, he penned this most wonderful

prayer for them. The pastor who prays genuinely from his heart for his congregation may confidently say to them, "Pray for me."

The prayer of the writer, as you observe, has overtones of the subject in which he had been engrossed. This epistle to the Hebrews is full of distinctions between the old covenant and the new one. The main idea of Hebrews is that the former covenant was only a foreshadowing of the dispensation that was to follow; it had only the shadow, and not the very image, of heavenly things. The writer's subject had been the covenant. When he prayed, his garments smelled sweetly of the myrrh and aloes and cassia (Psalm 45:8) among which his meditations had conducted him. He prayerfully expressed his desires according to his thought patterns. He wove into the texture of his prayer the meditations of his heart.

This is a very good method, especially when the prayer is public, for it ensures variety, it encourages unity, and it promotes edification. In fact, as the bee gathers nectar from many flowers to make honey, and the honey is often flavored with wild thyme or some other special flower that abounds in the region from where the bee collects its sweets, so do our souls gather dainty stores of the honey of devotion from all sources; but that upon which we linger the longest in our meditations yields a paramount savor and flavor to the expression and the spirit of our prayers. Nothing could have been more natural than that this discourse on the covenant was followed by this covenant prayer: *"The God of peace, that brought again from the dead our Lord Jesus, that great shepherd of the sheep, through the blood of the everlasting covenant, make you perfect in every good work to do his will."*

The subject of the epistle to the Hebrews is very deep, for it moves from the superficial fundamentals of the faith to those underlying truths that are more mysterious and profound. It is a book for the higher grade levels in Christ's school. Hence, this prayer is not for babes, but for men of understanding. Concerning this prayer, we could not say to all believers, *"After this manner therefore pray ye"* (Matthew 6:9), for they would not understand what they were asking. They would need to begin with something simpler, such as that beautiful *"Our Father which art in heaven"* (v. 9), which was Christ's original model of prayer, and which suits all believers alike.

Mature men eat strong meat, think sublime thoughts, and offer mighty prayers. As we may admire the prayer of the child in its simplicity, and the prayer of the young man in its vitality, so we may rejoice in the depth, extent, and sublimity of the prayer of one who has become a father in Christ (1 Corinthians 4:15) and feeds upon the covenant. All of these characteristics we find in this prayer, and thus we may safely infer that the writer was a spiritually mature father in the faith.

I invite those who want to understand the deep things of God to ask the Holy Spirit's assistance while we follow the writer of Hebrews in his covenant prayer—a prayer of which the covenant is the thread, the substance, and the plea. Our broader subject, therefore, is the covenant of grace, as it is referred to here.

THE NAMES OF THE COVENANT

I will begin by first reviewing the covenantal names the writer used. He called the ever blessed Father, who is one party of the covenant, *"the God of peace."* To the Redeemer, who has taken responsibility for fulfilling the other half of the covenant, he gave the title, *"our Lord Jesus, that great shepherd of the sheep."*

Dear friends, those of us who have believed in the Lord Jesus Christ are in Christ. He is our Head and Representative, our Shepherd and Sponsor. On our behalf, He made a covenant with the Father along these lines: since we *"were dead in* [our] *trespasses and sins"* (Ephesians 2:1), Christ promised that He would make full recompense to injured justice, so that the law of God would be fully honored; and the Father stipulated that He would grant full pardon, acceptance, adoption, and eternal life to us. The covenant has been completely satisfied on our part by Christ. Our text assures us of that, because, in fulfillment of His promise, Jesus has shed His blood.

"The God of Peace"

Now, the covenant only needs to be fulfilled on God's part by the eternal Father. In that aspect of the covenant, the writer of Hebrews called the Father, *"the God of peace."* What a precious name! Under the covenant of works, He is the God of vengeance: *"For the LORD thy God is...a jealous God"* (Deuteronomy 4:24), who will *"execute vengeance upon the heathen, and punishments upon the people"* (Psalm 149:7). To sinners He is the thrice-holy God, *"terrible out of* [His] *holy places"* (Psalm 68:35), and even *"a consuming fire"* (Hebrews 12:29). Yet to us, seeing that the covenant has been fulfilled on our side by our great Head and Representative, He is *"the God of peace."*

Christian, all is peace between you and God. No previous grounds for quarreling remain, nor should you ever fear that a new one can arise. The everlasting covenant secures everlasting peace between you and God. He is not the God of a hollow truce, not the God of a patched-up forgetfulness of unforgiven injuries, but *"the God of peace"* in the very deepest sense. He is Himself at peace, for there is a *"peace of God, which passeth all understanding"* (Philippians 4:7).

Moreover, by reason of His mercy, His people are made to enjoy peace of conscience within themselves. Thus, you feel that God is reconciled to you. Your heart rests in Him. Your sins, which separated you, have been removed. Perfect love has cast out all fear, which has torment (1 John 4:18).

While the Lord is at peace with Himself, and you are made to enjoy inward peace through Him, He is also at peace with you, for He loves you with a love unsearchable; He sees nothing in you but that which He delights in. In the covenant of grace, He does not look at you as you are in and of yourself, but as you are in your Surety, Christ Jesus. To the eye of God, there is no sight in the universe as lovely as His own dear Son, and His people in His Son. There is enough beauty in Jesus to make God forget our deformities, enough merit in Jesus to engulf our demerits, and sufficient efficacy in the atoning blood of our Great High Priest to wash away all our transgressions.

As for us, our souls, recognizing Christ's atoning blood and perceiving the love of God toward us, no longer experience war with God. We rebelled once, for we hated Him. Even now, when our old natures champ at the bit, and the Lord's will runs counter to our desires, we do not find it easy to bow before Him and say, *"I thank thee, O Father, Lord of heaven and earth, because...it seemed good in thy sight"* (Matthew 11:25–26). But yet, the new nature that has come to the forefront rules and governs, and all heart-contests between the soul and God have ended. In the broadest and most perfect sense, the Lord is to us, *"the God of peace."*

Oh, how I love that name, *"the God of peace."* He is Himself the peaceful, joyful God, unruffled, undisturbed; and we within ourselves are made to enjoy *"the peace of God, which passeth all understanding,* [which keeps our] *hearts and minds through Christ Jesus"* (Philippians 4:7). God is at peace with us, declaring that He will never be wrathful toward us or rebuke us, and we are rejoicing in Him, delighting in His law, and living for His glory. Henceforth, may it be that in every anxious hour, we look to the Lord by this cheering name, *"the God of peace,"* for as such the covenant reveals Him.

"Our Lord Jesus"

The writer of Hebrews had a view of the other great party to the covenant; he named Him *"our*

Lord Jesus." We must know the Redeemer first as *"Jesus,"* our Savior, who leads us into the promised eternal *"rest"* (Hebrews 4:1), the spiritual Canaan that has been given to us by the covenant (Exodus 6:4): *"there remaineth therefore a rest to the people of God"* (Hebrews 4:9).

Our Redeemer is also the *"Lord Jesus,"* in all the dignity of His nature, exalted *"far above all principality, and power"* (Ephesians 1:21), to be obeyed and worshipped by us. Moreover, He is *"our Lord Jesus"*: ours because He has given Himself to us, and we have accepted and received Him with holy delight as the Lord whom we cheerfully serve; ours because He saved us; ours because, by bringing us into His kingdom, He rescued us; and ours because we have a special relationship both to His sovereignty and His salvation.

We are not generally observant of the appropriateness of our Lord's names. We do not notice the instruction that was intended by the writers who used them, nor do we exercise enough discretion in our employment of them. Yet, there is great force in these titles when they are appropriately employed. Other names may be relatively insignificant, but in the titles of Jesus there is a wealth of meaning.

"That Great Shepherd of the Sheep"

Further, our Lord is called *"that great shepherd of the sheep."* In the covenant we are the sheep, and the Lord Jesus is the Shepherd. You cannot make a covenant with sheep; they do not have the ability to covenant. However, you can make a covenant with their Shepherd. Thus, glory be to God, although we like lost sheep had gone astray (Isaiah 53:6), we belonged to Jesus, and He made a covenant on our behalf and stood for us before the living God.

Now, I want to explain to you that in His death our Lord is the Good Shepherd: *"the good shepherd giveth his life for the sheep"* (John 10:11), and so He shows His goodness. In His resurrection He is the *"great shepherd,"* as we have it in the text, for His resurrection and return to glory display His greatness. Moreover, in the Second Advent He is the Chief Shepherd, and in this He shows His superior sovereignty: *"when the chief Shepherd shall appear"* (1 Peter 5:4), *"then shall ye also appear with him in glory"* (Colossians 3:4).

Our Lord was the "good" Shepherd in that He laid down His life for the sheep. There are other shepherds to whom He imparts His own goodness, who in His name feed His lambs and sheep. When He comes again the second time, He will appear with His undershepherds, as the Chief among them all. Yet, in His resurrection for our justification, in connection with the covenant, He is alone and bears the name of *"that great shepherd,"* of whom all prophecy has spoken, in whom all the divine decrees are fulfilled, before whom all others shrink away. He stands alone in that covenant capacity as the one and only Shepherd of the sheep.

It is very beautiful to trace the shepherds through the Old Testament. We can see Christ represented in Abel, the witnessing shepherd, pouring out the *"blood* [that] *crieth unto* [God] *from the ground"* (Genesis 4:10); in Abraham, the separating shepherd, leading his family flock into a strange country where they dwelt alone (Hebrews 11:9); in Isaac, the quiet shepherd, digging wells for his flock (Genesis 26:18) and feeding them in peace in the midst of his enemies; and in Jacob, the shepherd who was the surety for his sheep, who earned them by long toil and weariness (Genesis 29:20, 30).

There, too, we see our Lord in Joseph, the head shepherd over Egypt for the sake of Israel, of whom his dying father said, *"From thence is the shepherd, the stone of Israel"* (Genesis 49:24). Our Lord Jesus is now *"the head over all things* [for] *the church"* (Ephesians 1:22), the King who governs all the world for the sake of His elect, *"that great shepherd of the sheep"* who has all power committed into His hands for their sakes.

We can see Christ in Moses, the chosen shepherd, who led his people through the Red Sea, into the wilderness (Exodus 15:22), and up to the Promised Land (Exodus 16:35), feeding them with manna and giving them water from the rock that he struck (Exodus 16:32, 17:6). What a grand theme for reflection we have here! And then, there is David, the shepherd king and another type of Jesus, as he reigned in the covenanted inheritance over his own people, as a glorious king in the midst of them all. All these together enable us to see the varied glories of *"that great shepherd of the sheep."*

While we rest in the covenant of grace, we should view our Lord as our Shepherd and find solace in the fact that sheep have nothing to do with their own feeding, guidance, or protection. They have only to follow their shepherd to the pastures that he prepares, and all will be well with them. *"He maketh me to lie down in green pastures: he leadeth me beside the still waters"* (Psalm 23:2).

Beloved, this is a great subject, and I can only hint at it. Let us rejoice that our Shepherd is *"great,"* because He will be able to preserve all of His large flock from the great dangers that they will have to face. *"Yea, though I walk through the valley of the shadow of death, I will fear no evil: for thou art with me; thy rod and thy staff they comfort me"* (v. 4). He will be able to perform for them the great transactions with the great God that are demanded of a Shepherd of such a flock as that which Jesus calls His own. Under the covenant of grace, Jesus is Prophet, Priest, and King—a shepherd should be all this to his flock—and He is great in each of these offices.

THE SEAL OF THE COVENANT

The second major point for our consideration is the writer's reference to the covenant seal in our text: *"The God of peace that brought again from the dead our Lord Jesus, that great shepherd of the sheep, through the blood of the everlasting covenant."* The seal of the covenant is the blood of Jesus.

In ancient times, when men made covenants with one another, they generally used some kind of ceremony or exchange to bind and seal the bargain, as it were. Now, covenants with God are always confirmed with blood. As soon as blood has been shed and the victim has died, the agreement is forever established.

The Binder of the Covenant

When our heavenly Father made a covenant with Jesus Christ on our behalf, that covenant was true and firm: *"I will make an everlasting covenant with you, even the sure mercies of David"* (Isaiah 55:3). However, to make it stand eternally, blood had to be shed. Now, the blood ordained to seal the covenant was not *"the blood of bulls and of goats"* (Hebrews 10:4), but the blood of the Son of God Himself. This has made the covenant so binding that *"it* [would be] *easier for heaven and earth to pass, than one tittle of the* [covenant] *to fail"* (Luke 16:17).

God must keep His own promises. He is a free God, but He bound Himself:

> [13] *When God made promise to Abraham, because he could swear by no greater, he sware by himself,*
> [16] *For men verily swear by the greater: and an oath for confirmation is to them an end of all strife.*
> [17] *Wherein God, willing more abundantly to show unto the heirs of promise the immutability of his* [promise], *confirmed it by an oath:*
> [18] *That by two immutable things, in which it was impossible for God to lie, we might have a strong consolation.* (Hebrews 6:13, 16–18)

As soon as Christ's blood was shed to seal the covenant of grace, God was bound by His oath to bestow covenant blessings upon the flock that the Great Shepherd represented.

Beloved, as honest people, you and I are bound by our word. If we were to take an oath, which I trust we would not, we would certainly feel doubly bound by it. Moreover, if we had lived in the old times and blood had been sprinkled on a contract that we had made, we would respect the solemn sign and never even think of turning back from it.

Consider, for a moment, how impossible it would be for God to ever break that covenant of grace, which He voluntarily made with His own Son, and with us in Him, after it had been sprinkled with blood from the veins of His own beloved Son. No, the covenant is everlasting. It stands true forever, because it is confirmed by blood that is none other than the blood of the Son of God.

The Satisfaction of the Covenant Terms

Remember, too, that in our case, Christ's blood not only confirmed the covenant, but actually satisfied its terms. The stipulations of the covenant went like this: Christ must suffer for our sins and honor the divine law. He had kept the law in His life, but it was necessary, if He were to completely fulfill His part of the covenant, that He should also be *"obedient unto death, even the death of the cross"* (Philippians 2:8). Therefore, the shedding of His blood was the carrying out of His promised obedience to its utmost. It was the actual satisfaction of Christ's part of the covenant on our behalf. Thus, the whole covenant must now stand firm, for that upon which it depended is finished forever. It is not only ratified with that bloody signature, but by that blood it is actually accomplished on Christ's part. It cannot be that the eternal Father should turn back from His side of the compact, since our part of it has been carried out to the letter by *"that great shepherd of the sheep"* who laid down His life for us.

The Blood of the New Testament

By the shedding of blood, the covenant was turned into a testament. As the Scriptures say, *"For this is my blood of the new testament, which is shed for many for the remission of sins"* (Matthew 26:28), and, *"For where a testament is, there must also of necessity be the death of the testator"* (Hebrews 9:16).

In some Bibles, the marginal notes give "testament" as an alternate translation for *covenant*. We scarcely know how to translate the word in some Scripture passages, whether to say the new testament or the new covenant. Certainly it is now a testament: since Christ has kept His part of the covenant, He wills to us what is due to Him from God. Further, He bequeaths to us by His death all that comes to Him as His reward, making us His heirs by a testament that is rendered valid by His death. So, you may say "testament" if you please, or "covenant" if you will; but do not forget that His shed blood has made both testament and covenant sure and everlasting to all the sheep of whom Jesus is the Shepherd.

The Eternal Seal of the Covenant

Dwell with pleasure upon that phrase *"everlasting covenant."* Certain men in these days declare that *"everlasting"* does not mean everlasting, but indicates a period to which an end will come sooner

or later. I have no sympathy with them whatever.
Neither do I have any inclination to renounce the
eternal nature of heaven and other divine blessings
in order to gratify the tastes of wicked men who
wish to deny the eternity of future punishments.
Human nature leans in that direction, but the Word
of God does not. Following its unerring direction, we
rejoice in the everlasting covenant, which will abide
forever and ever.

The covenant of works is gone. Since it was
based on human strength and ability, it necessarily
dissolved as a dream. Given the nature of mankind,
it could not be everlasting. Man could not keep its
conditions, and so it fell by the wayside. However,
the covenant of grace depended only upon the power
and love and faithfulness of Christ, who has obedi-
ently fulfilled His part of the covenant. Therefore,
the covenant now rests only upon God, who remains
"faithful: he cannot deny himself" (2 Timothy 2:13).
Since *"he sware by himself"* (Hebrews 6:13), His word
cannot fail.

> As well might He His being quit,
> As break His promise, or forget.

*"His mercy is everlasting; and his truth en-
dureth to all generations"* (Psalm 100:5). He has
said, *"I will make an everlasting covenant with them,
that I will not turn away from them, to do them
good"* (Jeremiah 32:40). Therefore, do them good He
must, for *"God is not a man, that he should lie; neither the son of man, that he should repent"*
(Numbers 23:19). So then, the covenant seal of
Christ's blood makes all things sure.

THE FULFILLMENT OF THE COVENANT

Now, let us explore the fulfillment of the covenant, for God has begun to carry out His part in it. *"The God of peace, that brought again from the dead our Lord Jesus, that great shepherd of the sheep, through the blood of the everlasting covenant."*

First, Jesus Christ has been brought back from the dead by the Almighty through the blood of the covenant. Here is the story. Jesus was the Covenanter on our behalf; He took our sin upon Himself and undertook to suffer for it. Having been crucified, He yielded up His life. From the cross He was taken to the grave, and there He lay, imprisoned in death. Now, it was a term of the covenant on God the Father's part that He would not leave Christ's *"soul in hell, neither...suffer* [His] *Holy One to see corruption"* (Acts 2:27); this agreement has been faithfully kept.

Christ on the cross represented all of us who believe in Him, for we were crucified in Him. Jesus in the tomb also represented us, for we were buried with Him. Whatever happened to Him also happened to His flock. Now, then, what occurred to the body of Jesus? Did God keep His covenant? Did the worm devour that lovely frame, or did it defy corruption? Did it come to pass that He who descended into the earth never returned?

Wait for the dawning of the third day! Now, the promised time has come. As yet no worm dared to feed upon that godlike form, yet it lay among the dead. But on that glorious morning, the Slumberer awakened like one who has been refreshed with sleep. He arose. The stone was rolled away. Angels escorted Him to liberty. He came into the open air of the garden and spoke to His disciples.

Jesus who bled left the dead, no more to die. He waited for forty days so that He might let His friends see that He was really risen, but He had to rise higher still to be brought fully back to His former honors. Would God be faithful to Him and bring Him back from the dead, all the way from where He once had descended? Yes, for on the Mount of Olives, when the time came, He started to ascend. Cleaving the atmosphere, He mounted from amid His worshipping disciples, until a cloud received Him. But, did He rise fully to the point from which He had come? Did He in His own person gain for His church a full recovery from all the ruin of the Fall? Oh, see Him as He entered the gates of pearl! How He was welcomed by the Father! See how He climbed aloft and sat upon the Father's throne, for *"God also hath highly exalted him, and given him a name which is above every name: that at the name of Jesus every knee should bow"* (Philippians 2:9).

Now note by what means our Lord returned from the dead to all this glory. It was because He had presented the blood of the everlasting covenant. When the Father saw that Jesus had kept His part of the covenant, even to death, then He began to fulfill His portion of the contract by bringing back His Son from the grave to life, from shame to honor, from humiliation to glory, from death to immortality. And so, Jesus Christ *"sat down on the right hand of God; from henceforth expecting till his enemies be made his footstool"* (Hebrews 10:12–13).

Now, what has been done to Jesus has been virtually done to all His people, because *"the God of peace...brought again from the dead,"* not the Lord Jesus as a private person only, but *"our Lord Jesus,"* as *"that great shepherd of the sheep."* The sheep are with the Shepherd. Shepherd of the sheep, where is Your flock? We know that You have loved them even to the end, but You are gone. Have You left them in the wilderness? It cannot be, for thus it is written: *"Who shall separate us from the love of Christ?"* (Romans 8:35). Hear the Shepherd say, *"Father, I will that they also, whom thou hast given me, be with me where I am"* (John 17:24). *"Because I live, ye shall live also"* (John 14:19). *"Where I am, there shall also my servant be"* (John 12:26). Beloved, the sheep never are away from *"that great shepherd of the sheep."* They are always in His hand, and none can snatch them out of His hold (John 10:28). They were on earth with Him, and they are risen with Him.

If Jesus had remained in the grave, all His sheep would have perished there, too. However, when the Father brought Him back by the blood, He brought us back by the blood. In this He gives us the *"lively hope"* (1 Peter 1:3) that our souls will never die and the joyous expectation of resurrection for our bodies.

> For though our inbred sins require
> Our flesh to see the dust,
> Yet as the Lord our Shepherd rose,
> So all His followers must.

Jesus in heaven is there as our Representative, and His flock is following Him. I wish you could get a picture in your mind of the hills of heaven rising up from these lowlands called earth. We are feeding here a while under His watchful eye, and at a distance is a river that flows at the foot of the celestial hills and separates us from the heavenly pastures. One by one, our beloved ones are being called across the waters by the Good Shepherd's voice, and they cross the river pleasantly at His bidding, so that a long line of His sheep may be seen going over the stream and up the hillside to where the Shepherd stands and receives them. This line joins the upper flock to the lower and makes them all one company. Do you not see them continually streaming up to Him and proceeding under the direction of God, who tells them to be fed by the Lamb and to lie down forever where wolves can never come?

Thus, the one flock is even now with the Shepherd, for it is all one pasture to Him, although to us it seems divided by Jordan's torrent. Every one of the sheep is marked with the blood of the everlasting covenant. Every one of them has been preserved because Jesus lived. And as He was brought again from the dead by the Almighty through His shed blood, even so must they be, for so the covenant stands.

Remember, then, dear friends, that the punishment of the flock was borne by the Shepherd, that the flock died in the Shepherd, and that the flock now lives because the Shepherd lives. The life of the flock is consequently a new life. Remember, also, He will bring all His sheep that as yet are not called, out of their death in sin, even as He was brought out of His own death; He will lead onward and upward those who are called, even as He went onward and upward from the grave to the throne; He will preserve them all their journey through, even as He was preserved by the blood of the everlasting covenant; and He will perfect them even as He is perfect. Even as the God of peace has glorified His Son, so also will He bring all His chosen to eternal glory with Him.

THE GREAT BLESSING OF THE COVENANT

Next, let us delve into the blessing of the covenant that we find in on our text. What is one of the greatest of the covenant blessings? The writer of this epistle pleaded for it: *"Now the God of peace...make you perfect in every good work to do his will, working in you that which is wellpleasing in his sight."* Notice that one of the principal blessings of the new covenant is the power and will to serve God. The old covenant said, "There are the tablets of stone; make sure that you obey every word that is written on them. If you do, you will live, and if you do not, you will die." Man never did obey, and consequently no one ever entered heaven or found peace by the law.

However, the new covenant is drawn up this way: *"I will put my laws into their hearts, and in their minds will I write them; their sins and iniquities will I remember no more"* (Hebrews 10:16–17), and, *"I will put my fear in their hearts, that they shall not depart from me"* (Jeremiah 32:40). The prophets enlarged on this new covenant most instructively. It is not a covenant of "If you will, I will," but rather, "I will do, and you shall be."

As a covenant, this exactly suits me. If there were something to be performed by me, I could never be sure that I had fulfilled its terms, but since it is finished, I am at rest. God sets us working, and we work; but the covenant itself depends wholly upon that great promise: *"I will not turn away from them, to do them good"* (Jeremiah 32:40).

Thus, it was right for the writer of Hebrews to pray that God would *"make* [us] *perfect in every good work to do his will,"* because from ancient times this was the master promise: that those for whom Jesus died should be sanctified, purified, and equipped to serve their God. *"For we are his workmanship, created in Christ Jesus unto good works, which God hath before ordained that we should walk in them"* (Ephesians 2:10). Great as the prayer is, it is only asking what the covenant itself guarantees.

Fully Equipped for Service

Taking the text word by word, I see that the first blessing asked for by the writer is the ability for divine service. The Greek word *katartizo,* translated here as *"make you perfect,"* does not have the same meaning of *perfect* in the sense that we use it today; rather, it means "equipped," "fit," "prepared," "able." With this observation, I am not making any reference to the persistent debate about the doctrine of perfection. No one text could decide that controversy. I simply am stating a matter of fact. The expression should be rendered, "make you fully complete," or "fully equipped" to do His will. We ought to request earnestly that we may be qualified, adapted, and suited to be used by God for the performance of His will.

After a man, once dead in sin, is made alive again, the question arises, Who should be his master? To whom should we, having died in our Great Shepherd and having been brought again from the dead, yield ourselves? Certainly unto God alone. Our prayer is that we may be fully enabled to do His will. Our Shepherd did His Father's will, for He cried, *"I delight to do thy will, O my God"* (Psalm 40:8). *"By the which will we are sanctified"* (Hebrews 10:10), and each one of us is henceforth sanctified so that we may do that same will.

It is a grand desire, but it burns in every Christian's heart, that he may be prepared to serve his God, may be a vessel such as God can use, an instrument fit for the divine hand—weak and feeble, but not impure; unsuitable due to a lack of innate strength, but suitable through having been cleansed by the blood of the covenant. Dear brothers and sisters, ask for ability for service. Pray day and night that you may be *"meet for the master's use, and prepared unto every good work"* (2 Timothy 2:21).

An Inward Work of Grace

The writer of Hebrews was praying not merely for the ability for service, but moreover for an inward work of grace: *"working in you that which is wellpleasing in his sight."* I long above everything to possess more clearly in myself the inworking of the Holy Spirit. There is so much superficial religion, and we are so apt to be contented with it. Thus, it will enrich us to pray for deep heart work. We need to have our affections elevated, our wills subdued, our minds enlightened, and our entire beings deeply spiritualized by the presence of the Holy Spirit.

This is the promise of the covenant: *"God hath said, I will dwell in them, and walk in them"* (2 Corinthians 6:16). Remember, God worked in Christ in the grave by quickening His body to life, and He must work in us, *"according to the working of his mighty power, which he wrought in Christ, when he raised him from the dead"* (Ephesians 1:19–20).

Ask the Lord to do it in you. Do not be satisfied with a little, weak, almost imperceptible pulse of religion, of which you can hardly judge whether it is there or not. Instead, ask to feel the divine energies working within you. Keep asking to experience the eternal omnipotence of God, struggling and striving mightily in your spirit, until sin is conquered and grace gloriously triumphs. This is a covenant blessing. Seek for it.

An Outward, Visible Change

However, we need to be worked on outwardly as well as inwardly by God's Spirit. *"Working in you that which is wellpleasing in his sight"* is no small matter when you remember that nothing but perfect holiness can please God. Paul wanted each of us to be *"a vessel unto honour, sanctified, and meet for the master's use, and prepared unto every good work"* (2 Timothy 2:21).

Jesus expressed His desire to equip us to be versatile people who can do *"every good work,"* in this way: *"Verily, verily, I say unto you, He that believeth on me, the works that I do shall he do also; and greater works than these shall he do"* (John 14:12). He wishes us to be qualified for any station and every position.

When Jesus Christ rose from the dead, He was seen. There was not merely a secret quickening in Him, but a visible life. He was seen by angels and by men. Here on earth He lived for a period of time, being observed by all eyewitnesses. Just so, dearly beloved, there ought to be in us not only an inner resurrection that we feel, but also such a quickening that we are clearly alive to *"walk in newness of life"* (Romans 6:4). We must know the power of our Lord's resurrection and exhibit it in every action of our lives. May God grant us this, and may you know it by experience.

The Completeness of the Blessing

Next, let us observe the completeness of this covenant blessing. Just as Jesus has been fully restored to the place from which He came and has lost no dignity or power by having shed His blood, but rather has been exalted higher than ever, so God's design is to make us as pure and holy as Adam was initially. Likewise, He intends to add to our characters a force of love that never would have been there if we had not sinned and been forgiven—an energy of intense devotion, a strength of perfect self-sacrifice that we never could have learned if it had not been for *"Christ* [who] *hath loved us, and hath given himself for us"* (Ephesians 5:2).

God means to make us princes of the royal bloodline of the universe and court attendants of the

Lord of Hosts. He desires to fashion an order of beings who will come very near to Him, and yet will feel the humblest reverence for Him. They will be like Himself, *"partakers of the divine nature"* (2 Peter 1:4), and yet the most obedient of servants; perfectly free agents, and yet bound to Him by bonds that will never let them disobey in thought, in word, or in deed.

This is how He is fashioning the central battalion who will obey His eternal marching orders forever: He is forgiving us great sins; He is bestowing upon us great blessings; He is making us one with His dear Son; and when He has entirely freed us from our shrouds of death, He will call us up to where Jesus is, and we will serve Him with an adoration superior to all the rest of His creatures. Angels and seraphim cannot love as much as we will be able to, for they have never tasted His redeeming grace and His dying love. This high devotion is the Lord's aim for us.

God did not raise the Lord Jesus from the dead so that He might live a common life. He lifted Him up so that Christ might *"be the head over all things to the church,"* and that *"all things* [might be] *under his feet"* (Ephesians 1:22). Even so, the destiny of Christians is mysteriously sublime. They will not be lifted up from their natural deaths to a mere morality; they are destined to be something more than philanthropists and men esteemed by their peers. They are to exhibit to angels and principalities and powers the wonderful grace of God, showing in their own persons what God can do with His creatures through the death of His Son.

THE DOXOLOGY OF THE COVENANT

We conclude this study with the covenant doxology: *"To whom be glory for ever and ever. Amen."* If anything in the world can make a man praise his God, it is the covenant of grace, and the knowledge that he is included in it.

I ask you to think over the love of God in the covenant. It does not belong to all of you. Christ is not the Shepherd of the whole flock of men; He is only the Shepherd of the sheep, and He has not entered into any covenant for all mankind, but for His sheep alone. The covenant is for His own people. If you believe in Him, it is a covenant for you; but if you reject Him, you can have no participation in this covenant, for you are under the covenant of works, which condemns you.

But now, believer, for a moment think over this exceeding mercy. Your God, the everlasting Father, has entered into a solemn compact with Christ on your behalf, that He will save you, keep you, and make you perfect. He has saved you; in that act He has performed a large part of the covenant in you already. He has placed you in the path of life and kept you there to this day.

Further, if you are indeed His, He will keep you to the end. The Lord is not as the foolish man who began to build but was unable to finish. He does not commence to carry out a design and then turn from it. He will continue His work until He completes it in you: *"Being confident of this very thing, that he which hath begun a good work in you will perform it until the day of Jesus Christ"* (Philippians 1:6).

Can you really believe it? With you, a poor puny mortal, who will soon sleep in the grave—with you He has made an everlasting covenant! Will you not say with our text, *"To whom be glory"*? Like David on his deathbed, you can say, *"Although my house be not so with God; yet he hath made with me an everlasting covenant, ordered in all things, and sure"* (2 Samuel 23:5). I am sure you will joyfully add, "Glory be to His name."

Exclusive Glory

Our God deserves exclusive glory. Covenant theology glorifies God alone. There are other theologies everywhere that magnify men. They give him a finger in his own salvation, and so leave him a reason for throwing his cap up in the air and saying, "Well done, self!" But covenant theology puts man aside and makes him a debtor and a receiver. It does, as it were, plunge him into the sea of infinite grace and unmerited favor. It makes him give up all boasting, stopping the mouth that could have boasted by filling it with floods of love, so that it cannot utter a conceited word. A person saved by the covenant must give all the glory to God's holy name, for to God all the glory belongs. In salvation by the covenant, the Lord has exclusive glory.

Endless Glory

God also has endless glory. *"To whom be glory for ever and ever."* Have you glorified God a little, dear friends, because of His covenant mercy? Go on glorifying Him. Did you serve Him well when you were young? Oh, not as well as you wish you had, I know, but serve Him better now in these riper days. Throw yourself into the glorifying of God.

The task of saving yourself is not yours, for Jesus has done it all. You may sing,

> A charge to keep I have,
> A God to glorify—

However, you will not need to add these lines:

> A never-dying soul to save,
> And fit it for the sky.

That soul of yours is saved: He *"hath saved us and called us with an holy calling"* (2 Timothy 1:9). You have been made fit for the sky by the blood of the everlasting covenant: *"Thanks* [be] *unto the Father, which hath made us meet to be partakers of the inheritance of the saints in light"* (Colossians 1:12). All you have to do is to glorify the Lord who has saved you, *"set* [your] *feet upon a rock"* (Psalm 40:2), and established your ways. Now, glorify Him with all your might.

Are you getting gray, dear brother? With all your experience, you ought now to glorify the Lord more than ever. You will soon be up in the land of the living. Do not praise the Redeemer any longer in a poor feeble way, for you have but a short time to remain here. When we ascend above the clouds, how we will magnify our covenant God! I am sure I will not feel my powers extensive enough, even in heaven, to express my gratitude for His amazing love. I do not wonder that the poet said,

> Eternity's too short
> To utter half His praise.

People find fault with that expression and say it is an exaggeration. How would you have the poets write? Is not hyperbole allowable to them? I might even plead that it is not an extravagant exaggeration, for neither time nor eternity can utter all the praises of the infinite Jehovah.

> **Oh, for a thousand tongues to sing**
> **Our great Redeemer's praise.**

Covenant Glory

This will be the sweetest note of all our music: that He made with us *"an everlasting covenant, ordered in all things, and sure"* (2 Samuel 23:5), the covenant with *"that great shepherd of the sheep,"* by which every sheep was preserved, kept, and brought into the rich pastures of eternal glory. We will sing of covenant love in heaven. Our last song on earth and our first in paradise will be of the covenant, the covenant sealed with blood.

How I wish Christ's ministers would increasingly spread this covenant doctrine throughout the world. He who understands the two covenants has found the heart of all theology, but he who does not know the covenants knows next to nothing of the Gospel of Christ. You would think, to hear some ministers preach, that salvation is all of works, that it is still uncertain who will be saved, that it is all a matter of *if*s and *but*s and *maybe*s. If you begin to give them *shall*s and *will*s and purposes and decrees and pledges and oaths and blood, they call you Calvinistic. Why, this doctrine was true long before Calvin was born! Calvin loved it as we do, but it did not come from him. Paul had taught it long before—no, the Holy Spirit taught it to us in the Word, and therefore we hold to it. Bringing this truth again to the forefront will be a grand thing for the church.

By God's good grace, we must live this doctrine as well as preach it. May *"the God of peace, that brought again from the dead our Lord Jesus, that great shepherd of the sheep, through the blood of the everlasting covenant, make you perfect in every good work to do his will."* Then He will have glory through the covenant and through you, both now and forever.

Chapter 6

Pleading the Covenant of Grace

Have respect unto the covenant.
—Psalm 74:20

The person who understands the science of pleading with God will succeed in prayer. *"Put me in remembrance: let us plead together"* (Isaiah 43:26) is His divine command. *"Come now, and let us reason together"* (Isaiah 1:18) is His sacred invitation. *"Produce your cause, saith the LORD; bring forth your strong reasons"* (Isaiah 41:21) is His accommodating direction as to how to become victorious in supplication. Pleading is wrestling: arguments are the holds, the feints, the throes, the struggles with which we grip and vanquish the covenant angel, as Jacob did long ago until he received of God. (See Genesis 32:24–28.)

The humble statement of our desires is not without its value, but to be able to give reasons and arguments why God should hear us is to offer potent, prevailing prayer. Among all the arguments that can be used in pleading with God, perhaps there is none stronger than this: *"Have respect unto the covenant."* Like Goliath's sword, we may say of it, *"There is none like that"* (1 Samuel 21:9). If we have God's word regarding something, we may well pray, "Do as You have said, for as a good man only needs to be reminded of his own word in order to be brought to keep it, even so is it with You, our faithful God. We only need to put You in remembrance of these things, because You will do them for us." Since He has given us more than His word—namely, His covenant, His solemn compact—we may surely, with the greatest composure of spirit, cry to Him, *"Have respect unto the covenant."* Then we may both hope patiently and wait quietly for His salvation.

I trust that I need not explain to you, for you are by this point well-grounded in the matter, that the covenant spoken of here is the covenant of grace. There is a covenant that we could not plead in prayer, the covenant of works, a covenant that destroys us, because we have broken it. The first Adam sinned, and the covenant was broken. We have continued in his perverseness, and that covenant condemns us. By the covenant of works none of us can be justified, because we still continue to break our portion of it and thus to bring upon ourselves wrath to the uttermost degree.

However, God has made a new covenant with the Second Adam, our federal Head, Jesus Christ our

Lord. This covenant is without conditions, except such conditions as Christ has already fulfilled; *"an everlasting covenant, ordered in all things, and sure"* (2 Samuel 23:5); a better covenant that now consists only of promises, which are after this fashion:

> [10] *I will be to them a God, and they shall be to me a people.* (Hebrews 8:10)

> [26] *A new heart also will I give you, and a new spirit will I put within you.* (Ezekiel 36:26)

> [8] *I will cleanse them from all their iniquity, whereby they have sinned against me; and I will pardon all their iniquities, whereby they have sinned, and whereby they have transgressed against me.* (Jeremiah 33:8)

This covenant of grace, which once had conditions in it, all of which our Lord Jesus fulfilled when He paid the penalty for our transgressions, made an end of sin, and brought in everlasting righteousness. Now the covenant is all of promise, and it consists of infallible and eternal *shall*s and *will*s, which remain the same forever.

We will first contemplate what is meant by the plea of our text: *"Have respect unto the covenant."* Next, we will consider from where it derives its force. Thirdly, we will discuss how and when we may plead it. Then, we will determine the practical inferences that we can draw from it.

THE MEANING OF THE PLEA

First of all, what is meant by the plea: *"Have respect unto the covenant"*? It must mean something like this: "Fulfill Your covenant, O God; let it not be null and void. You have said this and that; now do as You have said. You have been pleased by the solemn sanction of oath and blood to make this covenant with Your people. Now be pleased to keep it. *'Hath he said, and shall he not do it? or hath he spoken, and shall he not make it good?'* (Numbers 23:19). We are persuaded of Your faithfulness; let our eyes behold Your covenant commitments fulfilled."

This plea means, "Fulfill all the promises of the covenant," for indeed all the promises in the covenant are now available. *"For all the promises of God in* [Christ Jesus] *are yea, and in him Amen, unto the glory of God by us"* (2 Corinthians 1:20). They are all *"yea"* and *"Amen"* in Christ Jesus, to the glory of God by us; and I may say without being unscriptural that the covenant contains within its sacred charter every gracious word that has come from the Most High, either by the mouth of prophets or apostles, or by the lips of Jesus Christ Himself.

The meaning in this case would be: "Lord, keep Your promises concerning Your people. We are in need. Now, O Lord, fulfill Your promise that we *'shall not want any good thing'* (Psalm 34:10). Here is another of Your promises: *'When thou passest through the waters, I will be with thee'* (Isaiah 43:2). We are in rivers of trouble. Be with us now. Redeem Your promises to Your servants. Let them not stand in the Book as letters that mock us, but prove that You meant what You wrote and said. Let us see that You have power and will make good every jot and tittle of all You have spoken. Have You not said, *'Heaven and earth shall pass away, but my words shall not pass away'* (Matthew 24:35)? O Lord, have respect for the promises of Your covenant."

In the context of our text there is no doubt that the petitioner meant, "O Lord, prevent anything from turning aside Your promises." The people of God were then in a very terrible state. The temple was burnt, the assembly was broken up, the worship of God had ceased, and idolatrous emblems stood even in the Holy Place where once the glory of God had been manifested. The suppliant was pleading, "Do not allow the power of the enemy to be so great as to frustrate Your purposes or to make Your promises void." Likewise, we may pray: "O Lord, do not allow me to endure such temptation that I would fall. Do not permit such affliction to come upon me that I would be destroyed. Did You not promise that no temptation would overtake us but such as we are able to endure and that, with the temptation, there would be a way of escape (1 Corinthians 10:13)? Now, *'have respect unto the covenant,'* and so order Your providence that nothing will happen to us contrary to Your divine pledge."

This plea also means, "So order everything around us that the covenant may be fulfilled. Is Your church at a low ebb? Raise up in her midst men who will preach the Gospel with power, who will be the means of her uplifting. Creator of men, Master of human hearts, You who can circumcise human lips to speak Your word with power, do this. Let Your covenant with Your church—that You will never leave her—be fulfilled. The kings of the earth are in Your hands. All events are controlled by You. You order all things, from the minute to the immense.

Nothing, however small, is too small for Your purpose. Nothing, however great, is too great for Your rule. Manage everything so that, in the end, each promise of Your covenant will be fulfilled to all Your chosen people."

That, I think, is the meaning of the plea, *"Have respect unto the covenant."* "Lord, keep the covenant, and see that it is kept. Fulfill the promise, and prevent Your foes from doing evil to Your children." This is a most precious plea, assuredly.

THE SOURCE OF THE POWER OF THE PLEA

Let us see where this plea, *"Have respect unto the covenant,"* derives its forcefulness. Because it pleads the covenant, which is based in God's character, it has all of the power of the Almighty behind it.

The Truth of God

It derives its force, first, from the veracity of God. If a man makes a covenant, we expect a man to keep it; and a man who does not keep his covenant is not esteemed among his peers. If a man has given his word, that word is his bond. If a thing is solemnly signed and sealed, it becomes even more binding. The person who would go back on a covenant would be thought to have forfeited his character among men.

God forbid that we should ever think the Most High could be false to His word! It is not possible. He can do all things except this—He cannot lie (Numbers 23:19). It is not possible that He could ever be untrue. He cannot even change: *"I am the LORD, I change not"* (Malachi 3:6). *"The gifts and calling of God are without repentance"* (Romans 11:29); His word is irrevocable. He will not break His covenant or alter anything that has gone out of His lips (Psalm 89:34).

Thus, when we come before God in prayer for a covenant mercy, we have His truthfulness to support us. "O God, You must do this. You are sovereign: You can do as You will, but You have bound Yourself by bonds that hold Your majesty. You have said it, and it is not possible that You should go back on Your own word." How strong our faith ought to be when we have God's fidelity to lean on. What dishonor we do to our God by our weak faith, for it is virtually a suspicion of the faithfulness of our covenant God.

His Jealous Guarding of His Honor

Next, to support us in using this plea, we have God's sacred jealousy for His honor. He has revealed to us that He is a jealous God: *"The LORD, whose name is Jealous, is a jealous God"* (Exodus 34:14). He has great respect for His honor among the sons of men. Hence, this was Joshua's plea: "What will the enemy say? *'And what wilt thou do unto thy great name?'"* (Joshua 7:9).

Now, if God's covenant could be trifled with, and if it could be proven that He had not kept the promise that He made to His chosen ones, it would not only be a dreadful thing for us, but it would bring grievous dishonor upon His name. That will never happen. God is too pure and holy, and He is completely too honorable ever to go back on the word that He has given to His servants.

If I feel that my strength is almost gone and I am about to fall into the pit, I may still be assured that He will not allow me to perish utterly, or else His honor would be stained, for He has said, *"They shall never perish, neither shall any man pluck them out of my hand"* (John 10:28). He could easily give me up to my enemies so far as my just deserts are concerned, for I deserve to be destroyed by them. However, His honor is engaged to save the lowliest of His people, and He has said, *"I give unto them eternal life"* (v. 28). He will not, therefore, for His honor's sake, allow me to be the prey of the Adversary, but will preserve me, even me, unto the end, so that I may be found blameless in the day of my Lord (1 Corinthians 1:8). Here is a solid foundation for faith.

The Enduring Quality of the Covenant

The next reflection that should greatly strengthen us is the enduring character of the covenant. This venerable covenant was no transaction of yesterday; before the earth ever existed, this covenant was made. We may not refer to first or last in regard to God, but humanly speaking, we may express it this way: the covenant of grace was God's first thought. Although we usually put the covenant of works first since it was revealed first in order of time, yet the covenant of grace is indeed the older of the two. God's people were not chosen yesterday, but *"before the foundation of the world"* (Ephesians 1:4). The Lamb, slain to ratify that covenant, although slain many centuries ago, was actually slain in the divine purpose from before the foundation of the world (Revelation 13:8). It is an ancient covenant: there is no other covenant as ancient.

It is to God a covenant that He holds in high esteem. It is not one of His light thoughts, not one of those thoughts that led Him to create the morning dew that melts before the day has run its course, or to make the clouds that light up the setting sun with glory but which soon lose their radiance. Rather, it is one of His great thoughts; yes, it is His eternal thought, the thought out of His own innermost being—this covenant of grace.

And because it is so ancient, and to God a matter so important, when we come to Him with this plea in our mouths, we must not stagger *"at the promise of God through unbelief"* (Romans 4:20). Instead, we may open our mouths wide, for He will assuredly fill them. "Here is Your covenant, O God. By Your own purposeful, sovereign will, You did ordain of old a covenant in which Your very heart is laid bare and Your love, which is Yourself, is manifested. O God, have respect for it. Do as You have said, and fulfill Your promise to Your people."

The Endorsement of God's Word

Nor is this all. It is but the beginning. In one chapter or even one book, I would not have the space to show you all the reasons that give force to the plea, but here is one more. The covenant has upon it a solemn endorsement. There is the stamp of God's own word—that is enough. The very word that created the universe is the word that spoke the covenant. But, as if that were not sufficient, seeing we are so prone to unbelief, God has added to it His oath, and *"because he could swear by no greater, he sware by himself"* (Hebrews 6:13). It would be blasphemy to dream that the Eternal could be perjured. He has set His oath to His covenant, in order *"that by two immutable things, in which it was impossible for God to lie,"* He might give to the heirs of grace *"strong consolation"* (v. 18).

Sealed with the Blood of the Lamb

Moreover, this venerable covenant, having been confirmed by God's oath, was sealed with blood. Jesus died to ratify it. His heart's blood was sprinkled on that Magna Charta of the grace of God to His people. It is a covenant that the just God must now keep. Jesus has fulfilled our side of it by having executed to the letter all the demands of God upon man. Our Surety and Substitute simultaneously kept the law and suffered all that was due by His people on account of their breach of it. Now, will not the Lord be true to His own word and the everlasting Father be faithful to His own Son? How can He refuse to His Son *"the joy that* [He] *set before him"* (Hebrews 12:2) and the reward that He promised Him? *"He shall see his seed....He shall see of the travail of his soul, and shall be satisfied"* (Isaiah 53:10–11).

Beloved, the faithfulness of God to His covenant is not so much a matter between you and God as it is between Christ and God. It now stands that Christ, as the unblemished Advocate, puts in His claim before the throne of infinite justice for the salvation of every soul for whom He shed His blood, and He must have what He has purchased. Oh, what confidence there is in this! The rights of the Son, blended with the love and the veracity of the Father, cause the everlasting covenant to be *"ordered in all things, and sure"* (2 Samuel 23:5).

The Unfailing Nature of the Covenant

Further, keep in mind that nothing in the covenant has ever failed up until this very moment. The Lord's word has been tried by ten thousand times ten thousand of His people. They have been in perplexing emergencies and serious difficulties. Yet, it has never been reported in the gates of Zion that the promise has been invalidated; neither have any said that the covenant is null and void. Ask those who were before you, who passed through deeper waters than you. Ask the martyrs who gave up their lives for their Master, "Was He with you to the end?" The peaceful smiles upon their faces while enduring the most painful deaths were evident testimonies that God is true. Their joyous songs when being burned alive, their exaltation even while on the rack, and the clapping of their hands and their high praises when rotting away in loathsome dungeons—all these have proved how faithful the Lord has been.

And have you not heard with your own ears the testimony of God's people as they were dying? They were in conditions in which they could not have been sustained by mere imagination or buoyed up by delirium, and yet they were as joyful as if their dying day had been their wedding day. Death is too solemn a matter for a man to sustain a masquerade at that time. What did your wife say in death? Or your mother, who is now with God? Or your child, who had learned the Savior's love? Can you not recall their testimonies even now? I think I hear some of them. Among the things of earth that are most like the joys of heaven, I think this is one of the foremost—the joy of departing saints when they already hear the voices of angels hovering near, when they attempt to tell us in broken language of the joys that are bursting in upon them, as their sight is blinded by the excess of brightness and their hearts are enraptured with the bliss that floods them. Oh, it has been sweet to see true believers depart from this world!

I mention these things now, not merely to refresh your memories, but to establish your faith in God. He has been true so many times and never false. Should we now experience any difficulty in depending on His covenant? No, by all these many years in which the faithfulness of God has been put to the test and has never failed, let us be confident that He will still regard us, and let us pray boldly, *"Have respect unto the covenant."* Remember, "As it was in the beginning, it is now and ever shall be, world without end." It will be to the last believer as it was with the first. The testimony of the last soldier of the host will be this: *"According to all that he promised: there hath not failed one word of all his good promise"* (1 Kings 8:56).

The Gift of Faith in the Covenant

I have one more reflection here. Our God has taught many of us to trust in His name. We were long in learning the lesson, and nothing but Omnipotence could have made us willing to *"walk by faith, not by sight"* (2 Corinthians 5:7). With much patience the Lord brought us at last to have no reliance on ourselves, but only on Him. Now we depend solely on His faithfulness and His truth. Is that your case, beloved? What then? Do you think that God has given you this faith to mock you? Do you believe that He taught you to trust in His name and brought you thus far to put you to shame? Has His Holy Spirit given you confidence in a lie? Has He developed in you a false faith? God forbid! Our God is no demon that would delight in the misery that a groundless confidence would be sure to bring to us.

If you have faith, He gave it to you (Ephesians 2:8). He who gave it to you knows His own gift and will honor it. He has never been false yet, even to the feeblest faith. If your faith is great, you will find Him greater than your faith, even when your faith is at its greatest. Therefore, *"be of good cheer"* (Matthew 14:27). The fact that you believe should encourage you to say, "Now, O Lord, I have come to rest upon You; can You fail me? I, poor worm, know no confidence but in Your dear name; will You forsake me? I have no refuge but Your wounds, O Jesus, no hope but in Your atoning sacrifice, no light but in Your light; can You cast me off?"

It is not possible that the Lord would cast away one who thus trusts Him. *"Can a woman forget her*

sucking child, that she should not have compassion
on the son of her womb? yea, they may forget, yet will
I not forget thee" (Isaiah 49:15). Can any of us forget
our children when they fondly trust us and are dependent on us? No, we cannot, and neither can our
heavenly Father. The Lord is no monster: He is tender and full of compassion, faithful and true. Moreover, Jesus is our *"friend that sticketh closer than a
brother"* (Proverbs 18:24). The very fact that He has
given us faith in His covenant should help us to
plead, *"Have respect unto the covenant."*

APPLICATIONS OF THE COVENANT PLEA

Having thus shown you, dear friends, the
meaning of the plea and the source from which it
derives its power, I will now discuss some of the
practical considerations in pleading, *"Have respect
unto the covenant,"* such as how and when that
covenant may be pleaded.

When Being Convicted of Sin

First, it may be pleaded when you are under a
sense of sin, when your soul feels the weight of its
guiltiness. The author of the book of Hebrews reit-
erated the words of Jeremiah when he wrote this
about the covenant of grace:

> [10] *For this is the covenant that I will make with
> the house of Israel after those days, saith the
> Lord; I will put my laws into their mind, and
> write them in their hearts: and I will be to them a
> God, and they shall be to me a people:*

[11] *And they shall not teach every man his neighbour, and every man his brother, saying, Know the Lord: for all shall know me, from the least to the greatest.*
[12] *For I will be merciful to their unrighteousness, and their sins and their iniquities will I remember no more.* (Hebrews 8:10–12)

Now, dear friend, suppose that you are under a sense of sin, a burden of conviction. Perhaps something has revived in you a recollection of past guilt, or it may be that you have sadly stumbled this very day. Satan is whispering, "You will surely be destroyed, for you have sinned." Go to your heavenly Father, open your Bible to this passage, put your finger on that twelfth verse, and say, "Lord, You have in infinite, boundless, inconceivable mercy entered into covenant with me, a poor sinner, seeing that I believe in the name of Jesus. Now I plead with You, *'Have respect unto* [Your] *covenant.'* You have said, *'I will be merciful to their unrighteousness.'* O God, be merciful to mine. *'Their sins and their iniquities will I remember no more.'* Lord, remember no more my sins; forget forever my iniquity." This is the way to use the covenant: when you are under the conviction of sin, plead the clause in the covenant that meets your case.

When Desiring Holiness

But suppose, beloved brother or sister, you are striving to overcome inward corruption, with the intense desire that holiness be developed in you. Then, read the covenant again as you find it in the book of

Jeremiah. This is just another version of the same covenant of grace:

> ³³ *This shall be the covenant that I will make with the house of Israel; After those days, saith the* LORD, *I will put my law in their inward parts, and write it in their hearts.* (Jeremiah 31:33)

Now, can you not plead that and say, "Lord, Your commandments upon stone are holy, but I forget them and break them. O my God, write them on the fleshy tablets of my heart. Come now, and make me holy; transform me; write Your will upon my very soul, so that I may live it out and, from the warm impulses of my heart, serve You as You would be served. *'Have respect unto the covenant,'* and sanctify Your servant."

When Resisting Temptation

Or, suppose that you desire to be upheld when you are under strong temptation, lest you should slip back and return to your old ways. Take the covenant as you find it in the thirty-second chapter of Jeremiah. Meditate on these verses and learn them by heart, for they may be a great help to you one of these days.

> ³⁸ *And they shall be my people, and I will be their God:*
> ³⁹ *And I will give them one heart, and one way, that they may fear me for ever, for the good of them, and of their children after them:*
> ⁴⁰ *And I will make an everlasting covenant with them, that I will not turn away from them, to do*

them good; but I will put my fear in their hearts,
that they shall not depart from me.
                        (Jeremiah 32:38–40)

Now, *"come boldly unto the throne of grace"*
(Hebrews 4:15), and say, "O Lord, I am almost gone,
and people are telling me I will inevitably fall. But,
O my Lord and Master, here stands Your word. Put
a godly fear of You in my heart, and fulfill Your
promise, so that I will not depart from You." This is
the sure road to final perseverance.

In Any Kind of Need

In a similar way, I might take you through all
the various needs of God's people and show that, in
seeking to have them supplied, they may aptly cry,
"Have respect unto the covenant." For instance, suppose you were in great distress of mind and needed
comfort. You could go to Him with that covenant
promise, *"As one whom his mother comforteth, so*
will I comfort you" (Isaiah 66:13). Go to Him with
that and say, "Lord, comfort Your servant."

If there happens to be trouble plaguing the
church, how sweet it is that we are able to go to the
Lord and say, "Your covenant says this: *'The gates of*
hell shall not prevail against [Your church]'
(Matthew 16:18). O Lord, it seems as though they
would prevail. Interpose Your strength, and save
Your church."

Whenever you are seeking the conversion of the
ungodly, desiring to see sinners saved, and the world
seems so dark, look at our text again—the entire
verse—*"Have respect unto the covenant: for the dark*

places of the earth are full of the habitations of cruelty" (Psalm 74:20). To this you might add, "But, Lord, You have said that *'the earth shall be filled with the knowledge of the glory of the LORD, as the waters cover the sea'* (Habakkuk 2:14), and that *'all flesh shall see the salvation of God'* (Luke 3:6). *'Have respect unto the covenant,'* Lord. Help our missionaries, speed Your Gospel, command the mighty angel to fly through the midst of heaven to preach the everlasting Gospel to all who dwell on earth, to every nation and kindred and tongue and people" (Revelation 14:6). Why, this is a grand missionary prayer: *"Have respect unto the covenant."*

Beloved, the covenant plea is a two-edged sword, to be used in all conditions of strife, and it is a holy balm of Gilead that will heal all conditions of suffering.

THE OBVIOUS INFERENCE OF THE PLEA

And now, let us conclude with this last question, What is the obvious, practical inference for our lives from this plea, *"Have respect unto the covenant"*? Why, is it not that, if we ask God to have respect unto it, we ought to have respect for the covenant ourselves? There are several aspects of respect for the covenant that we each need to develop in our own lives.

A Grateful Respect

First, we need to have a grateful respect for it. Bless the Lord that He ever condescended to enter into covenant with you. What could He see in you even to give you a promise, much more to make a covenant with you? Blessed be His dear name that He condescended to covenant eternally with sinners such as we are. This is the sweet theme of our hymns on earth, and it will be the subject of our songs in heaven.

A Believing Respect

Next, we need to have a believing respect for it. If it is God's covenant, do not dishonor it with your doubt. The *"everlasting covenant* [stands], *ordered in all things, and sure"* (2 Samuel 23:5). May you be like Abraham, who *"staggered not at the promise of God through unbelief; but was strong in faith, giving glory to God"* (Romans 4:20).

> His every work of grace is strong
> As that which built the skies;
> The voice that rolls the stars along
> Speaks all the promises.

A Joyful Respect

Next, we need to have a joyful respect for the covenant. Get out your harps, and join in praise with David: *"Although my house be not so with God; yet he hath made with me an everlasting covenant, ordered in all things, and sure"* (2 Samuel 23:5). Here is enough to make a heaven in our hearts while we are yet on earth: the Lord has entered into a covenant of grace and peace with us, and He will bless us forever.

A Jealous Respect

Then, we need to have a jealous respect for it. Never allow the covenant of works to be mixed with the covenant of grace. Hate that preaching—I say no less than that—hate the preaching that does not discriminate between the covenant of works and the covenant of grace, for it is deadly preaching and damning preaching. You must always draw a straight, clear line between what is of man and what is of God, for *"cursed be the man that trusteth in man, and maketh flesh his arm"* (Jeremiah 17:5).

If you have begun with the Spirit under this covenant, do not think of being made perfect in the flesh under another covenant. Be holy under the precepts of the heavenly Father, but do not be legalistic under the taskmaster's lash. Do not return to the bondage of the law, for *"ye are not under the law, but under grace"* (Romans 6:14). *"Stand fast therefore in the liberty wherewith Christ hath made us free, and be not entangled again with the yoke of bondage"* (Galatians 5:1).

A Practical Respect

Finally, we need to have a practical respect for the covenant. Let others see that the covenant of grace, while it is your reliance, is also your delight. Be ready to speak of it to others. Be ready to show that the effect of its grace upon you is one that is worthy of God, since it has a purifying effect upon your life. *"Every man that hath this hope in him purifieth himself, even as he is pure"* (1 John 3:3).

Thus, *"have respect unto the covenant"* by conducting yourself in a way that one of God's elect should conduct himself.

The covenant says, *"Then will I sprinkle clean water upon you, and ye shall be clean: from all your filthiness, and from all your idols, will I cleanse you"* (Ezekiel 36:25). Do not love idols, then. Be clean, you covenanted ones.

May the Lord preserve you and make His covenant to be your boast on earth and your song forever in heaven. Oh, may the Lord bring us all into the bonds of His covenant and give us a simple faith in His dear Son, for that is the mark of the heirs of the covenant!